Qualitative Psychology:
Introducing Radical Research

Qualitative Psychology: Introducing Radical Research

Ian Parker

Open University Press

Open University Press
McGraw-Hill Education
McGraw-Hill House
Shoppenhangers Road
Maidenhead, Berkshire
England SL6 2QL

email: enquiries@openup.co.uk
world wide web: www.openup.co.uk

and Two Penn Plaza, New York, NY 1012–2289
USA

First published 2005

A catalogue record of this book is available from the British Library

ISBN 0 335 213499 (pb)   0 335 213502 (hb)

Library of Congress Cataloging-in-Publication Data
CIP data has been applied for

Typeset by BookEns Ltd, Royston, Herts.
Printed and bound in Great Britain by
Bell and Bain Ltd, Glasgow

Contents

List of boxes

Acknowledgements

One of the many fictions perpetrated in this book is that one single author could ever really be responsible for what lies within it. My name is on the cover, but I could not have written all this without the help of Mark Barratt, Alex Bridger, Erica Burman, Rose Capdevila, Khatidja Chantler, Gill Craig, Michele Crossley, Babak Fozooni, Thekla Giakeimi, Eugenie Georgaca, Brendan Gough, David Harper, Daniel Heggs, Derek Hook, Carolyn Kagan, Rebecca Lawthom, Sue Lewis, Ken McLaughlin, Tom Phillips, David Putwain, Judith Sixsmith, Carol Tindall, Justin Vaughan, Katherine Watson, Christian Yavorsky and Alexandra Zavos.

Preface

The first three chapters of this book – on theoretical assumptions, ethics and reflexivity – outline key conceptual issues that need to be thought through with respect to any method in psychology, whether qualitative or quantitative. The discussion in these three chapters emphasizes the role of theory in qualitative research, and you will find an outline of theoretical resources that I draw upon throughout the rest of the book in the first chapter on 'groundwork'. The chapters on ethics and reflexivity depart from the usual appeals to morality and authenticity in qualitative psychology, and you will find an argument for a quite different, theoretically grounded, approach to these questions.

The middle five chapters – on ethnography, interviewing, narrative, discourse and psychoanalysis – outline specific methodological approaches and contain examples of research to illustrate how the methods work in practice. The overall tone of these chapters is positive about the possibilities that different methods in qualitative psychology open up, and you will find descriptions of theoretical resources and suggestions about how the research may be undertaken. The first little boxes in these five chapters contain the negative comments I need to make about some of the problems with certain qualitative methods that are currently popular in psychology.

The final three chapters show how the methods I have described connect with action research (as something to be taken further) and with criteria and reporting of research (as obstacles and annoyances that we have to learn to find our way through). There are many 'stages' and 'points' itemized in the boxes that break up the argument in each chapter, and I must admit that there were times when I felt my brain sicken and stomach clench at the rather bureaucratic and formulaic structure of the text. Perhaps I have even reproduced the form of mainstream psychology and also, along the way, the mechanistic way the discipline likes to imagine the nature of human thinking. However, even though this book is not the most creative and imaginative alternative to psychology, it does set out steps towards creative and imaginative qualitative research, steps you can then kick away when you go on to do something better.

1 Groundwork

Qualitative research opens a space inside psychology to do something radically different to link human experience with social action.

A variety of qualitative psychology research groups and journals have sprung up in the last decade to claim and defend that space, and healthy debate is flourishing between devotees of different approaches. The Discourse Unit is but one site where never-ending internal disagreement has produced many alternative images of what psychology could be and a range of methodological innovations by which we might do psychology differently. This chapter draws on some of the theoretical resources that have been accumulating over the years in the Discourse Unit, in radical psychology and further afield (see Parker 2003a), but the most important battleground now is methodology in psychology. Why?

The discipline of psychology often busies itself with finding out what is wrong with people and putting things right, and to do that it has usually drawn on shared cultural representations of what 'normal' behaviour and cognitive functions are like. These ideas about pathology are so diverse, however, that it is sometimes difficult to see how they can coexist in the same institution, and the recent proposals for 'positive' psychology do not fare much better (cf. Holzman 1999). What has really held psychology together and defined it as a distinct discipline is its *method*, the way it goes about knowing those that it observes and regulates (Rose 1985). In its method psychology has helped to make its objects of study into the kind of 'subjects' who can be known, so the stakes of control and resistance are much more than simple images of what people are. This means that *radical research in qualitative psychology is the subversion and transformation of how we can come to know more about psychology*.

Methodological debate in qualitative research is thus a place where we can think through what is going on in the discipline and elaborate theoretical work that will both enable us to take some distance from psychology and produce a different kind of knowledge in a different way. Three aspects of this debate are crucial, and will recur as themes as we go along. First is the opportunity to address political differences in the field of research, to keep in mind the political impetus and effects of our work (Burman 1997). Second is attending to the way the process of research itself reproduces certain kinds of social relationships, and how research relationships might 'prefigure' something better (Kagan and Burton 2000). Third is awareness that every alternative methodological paradigm in psychology so far has been neutralized and absorbed so that its radical promise is betrayed (Burman 1996). That process of recuperation threatens to turn innovative methodology into mere technique. This chapter, in contrast, aims to encourage methodological innovation in every piece of research.

Four resources for the groundwork

We can get a better idea of what the 'political' stakes are in radical qualitative research – how it is that questions of methodology in psychology have to be seen as political questions – if we look at four theoretical resources in the Discourse Unit (Parker 2003a). I will highlight one key methodological point that arises from each of these resources.

- First, feminist theory has historically been the most important source of new ideas for qualitative methods in psychology, and this has been a consequence of the impact of feminism across the social sciences and as a political movement (e.g. Harding 1987). Since the 'second wave' feminism of the 1960s, a concern with women's oppression has opened up work on the different forms of oppression suffered by different kinds of women, and focused attention, for example, on 'race' and sexual orientation. The methodological implications of this shift of attention to varieties of oppression have been immense. On the one hand, the notion that 'the personal is political' emphasized the way the realm of individual experience and relationships operated to reproduce or challenge patterns of power (Rowbotham *et al.* 1979). Here is one reason why psychological knowledge should become part of feminist work. On the other hand – the key methodological point – feminism discovered again that *knowledge is different for the powerful than it is for the oppressed*. The argument that those with power are simply unable to see the mechanisms that privilege their own viewpoint over others is at the heart of feminist 'standpoint' theory (Hartsock 1987). The 'standpoint' of the oppressed gives women, and by implication members of other oppressed groups, a distinctive view of what is going on, and the 'standpoint' of a researcher working to the agenda of an academic institution, for example, may chime with or obscure that distinctive, perhaps more radical, view.

- Second is the impact of 'poststructuralist' or 'postmodern' theory in social and developmental psychology. The terms 'poststructuralism' and 'postmodernism' are rather misleading labels used to gather together a diverse group of French theorists, and they are sometimes used to underpin the activity of unravelling texts as a 'deconstruction' of how the texts are rhetorically structured (e.g. Burman 1994a). One of the most important figures in this motley crew is the historian Michel Foucault (1977, 1979), and there are profound implications for methodology in his work. He argued, for example, that historical accounts are always produced from the standpoint of present-day practices, usually with the function of legitimating the way we have come to do things or think about ourselves. Different disciplines (such as psychology) operate as 'regimes of truth' in which there is a circulation of knowledge about objects that are formed by the very practices through which they are known. This makes the way we produce knowledge as important, if not more so, than the actual things we think we have discovered. Although the position this leads to is sometimes confused with outright relativism – in which it does not seem to matter what we know – the methodological lesson is actually that how we know things is extremely important, so important that perhaps it is better if our starting point is to emphasize *the activity or process of research rather than the objects we attempt to know* (Newman and Holzman 1997).
- The third resource is psychoanalysis. This approach often seems even more dubious than psychology, and although psychologists tend to dislike psychoanalysis, they deal with it by making it seem as if it is trying to compete on the same ground as them to provide a 'scientific' explanation of human activity. However, although some forms of psychoanalysis in the English-speaking world have tried to turn it into a kind of psychology which would adapt people to society, genuine psychoanalysis is actually the reverse of psychology (Jacoby 1977). Whether we like it or not, one very good reason why we need to take psychoanalysis seriously is that images of 'egos', 'defences' and the 'unconscious' are a powerful part of the popular representation of what psychology is, and many people talk about themselves as if these things are true, to the extent that they become true for them in contemporary 'psychoanalytic culture' (Parker 1997). This effect of psychoanalysis – that it becomes true for people through being repeated as a discourse and used by them to talk about themselves – then draws attention to the way that *all forms of psychology – whether cognitive, developmental or forensic – also*

come to work because they are repeated so many times. They then come to acquire meaning for us and we become attached to those meanings. One key methodological lesson from psychoanalysis, in addition, is that whatever 'objective' standpoint we adopt is suffused with our own interests and fantasies; here is more support for the argument that 'objectivity' is a form of 'subjectivity' (Hollway 1989).

- Fourth, finally, is Marxism, which has a distinctive view of reality as something that emerges historically through contradiction, a reality which changes through a process of tension and conflict between different social classes. One problem is that sometimes Marxism is used to talk about class struggle as if other forms of oppression are unimportant, despite the fact that there was much early work in the Marxist tradition on the relationship between public and private power (e.g., Engels 1884). A second problem is that sometimes Marxism in the social sciences is reduced to a methodological approach known as 'dialectical materialism', an approach which was turned into ideological mystification by the bureaucrats working under Stalin and his successors in the Soviet Union from the late 1920s. However, there is a rich variety of traditions in Marxism that aim to connect with other visions of understanding and emancipation, and there are many different ways of connecting these traditions of Marxism with traditions in psychology (e.g. Parker and Spears 1996). A particularly important connection today is with studies of language and the 'social construction' of reality. Some of the studies using Foucault's work, for example, treat language as if it floats above reality, as if it cannot be analysed separately from it (cf. Hook 2001), and Marxism is now useful methodologically to insist that *the language we use is woven into reality, and that this reality is historically constructed so it can be transformed for the better.*

Feminism, Foucault, psychoanalysis and Marxism have each made an impact on psychology in the last two decades, and there have been some attempts to combine them with a view to 'changing the subject' (e.g. Henriques *et al.* 1984). As theoretical frameworks they go well beyond the four key methodological points I have extracted and highlighted here. But those methodological points – concerning standpoint, knowledge, objectivity and reality – will help us now to start working through how we might do psychological research differently.

In and against the discipline

Psychology is very good at turning people into things, and one of the ironies of modern psychological methods in the laboratory-experimental paradigm was that the people who were studied were called 'subjects' when they were actually treated like objects. In most quantitative research in psychology it is really the psychologist who is the subject, observing and measuring the behaviour of others.

This means that we have to take care to avoid falling into this comfortable and lazy research position. Instead, radical qualitative research needs to take seriously the idea that those we study are actually 'subjects' – even if we find them dangerous or disagreeable – and tackle head-on the fact that they are actively trying to make sense of what we do in any research study. There is no research without 'demand characteristics' or 'volunteer traits', and so we may as well turn those problems for traditional psychology into virtues in our own research (Parker 1994a). This does not mean, however, that we should patronize those we study by pretending to be empathic and respectful all the time. The ethos of this research is that while our position as researcher working from within an academic institution might be problematic – following agendas that we may have had no say in formulating – our political position demands that we do evaluate what is said and what we will do with it.

Some studies may deliberately turn the gaze of the discipline around so that instead of standing with the psychologist and observing the 'others' who are outside psychology, we will look at what the psychologists are doing. A good deal of research is still to be done on what psychology is doing to people (and many of the examples of research in this book are of this kind).

Whether this deliberate focus on psychology is the strategy you want to adopt or not, the three things that psychology usually does so well are things to be avoided here. First, we need to refuse to individualize the phenomena we are studying. Even when psychologists do bad things to others, for example, it is not usually because they are nasty people, but because they are institutionally positioned to do harm and because what they do has been legitimized by the history of psychology and the demands of the state to maintain order. Second, we need to refuse to essentialize the things we describe. Even when so much of the history of psychology is so patently a history of colonial power and the attempt by white psychologists to discover inferior mentalities in other peoples, it is not much more progressive to say that this behaviour is some deep wired-in drive for control than it was for the psychologists to resort to stories of instincts to essentialize psychological characteristics. Third, we need to refuse to psychologize as we provide explanations. This may be the most difficult thing to avoid, because there are so many powerful motifs outside the discipline of psychology that appear to provide alternative ways of explaining things but which still reduce things to 'prejudice', 'defensiveness' or 'false beliefs'. What people say about 'psychology' should be the beginning of the story for us, not the end point.

Box 1.1   *A problematic starting point: psychology*

The four alternative theoretical vantage points outlined in this chapter are useful methodologically, not only because they show us new ways of knowing about our own psychology but also because they show us why we would have been unable to get very far if we had taken the discipline of psychology as our starting point.

1   *Feminism* reveals psychology to be a stereotypically masculine enterprise – patriarchy – characterized by prediction and control of people so that they can be managed more efficiently, very suspicious of girly things like feelings that might escape or challenge 'facts' that have already been 'discovered'.

2   *Foucault* provides historical analyses of the way psychology functions as part of an apparatus of surveillance – the psy-complex – in which populations are known, and individuals come to sense that everything about their private behaviour and secret thoughts is observed.

3   *Psychoanalysis* interprets psychology as an overly-rationalist discipline – obsessional – preoccupied with putting everything neatly in place and shutting out anything unpleasant that does not seem to fit the systems of categories in its theories and research instruments.

4   *Marxism* demonstrates how psychology serves the needs of a particular political-economic system – capitalism – by isolating individuals from each other so that they compete for resources rather than question how their own creative capacities are alienated from them.

What should be noticed is that each of these vantage points opens up a different way of thinking about human action and experience that does not necessarily call for any alternative 'psychology' to be put in place of what they oppose. Rather, it is the realm of the psychological that is thrown into question as the explanation for anything of importance. Psychology is part of the story, but we need to know what the story is before we can get anywhere with it, and get beyond it.

The stories and subtexts of individuality

Here is the biggest problem. It would be relatively easy to challenge psychology if it was simply part of an apparatus of discipline and control, forcing people to conform and labelling people who refuse to fit the categories of what we understand today to be 'normal'. This very wide-ranging apparatus, the 'psy-complex' – which includes psychology, psychiatry, psychoanalysis, social work, governmental agencies concerned with how we should look after our children, and advice columns in newspapers and magazines concerning how we should manage our emotions and relationships – is much more complex than that however (Rose 1985).

The analysis of the psy-complex I use in this book takes up Foucault's (1977, 1979) historical work on the production of individuality in western culture, and emphasizes that the psy-complex works through both discipline and confession. That is, our 'subjects' are already ready to speak about themselves to us psychologists, and they expect that we want to hear about private thoughts and feelings, as if those things dredged up from under the surface will help us to explain why people do things. This is why the refusal of individualizing, essentializing and psychologizing assumptions and techniques in psychological research is so difficult. It is not only us the researchers that are tempted to do these things. Our 'subjects' are now more often than not the kind of subjects who *expect* us to do it to them.

So, the task of the qualitative researcher is to produce this kind of knowledge in a way that is different from this popular view, to enable accounts and modes of activity usually hidden from psychology to come to light.

Box 1.2   *Contexts for studying 'psychology'*

Psychology is so much bound up with everyday common-sense understandings of ourselves that it is sometimes difficult to step aside from assumptions that the discipline makes about those that it studies. This is why it is important to know that 'psychology' is very different in different cultures at different points in history. Knowing this can help us take some distance from what we think counts, and from how we think we should come to know it. These four instances of 'psychology', a selection from the many varieties there are, highlight how every approach carries within it certain political assumptions and consequences.

1   *Liberation psychology* emerged as a vision of emancipation from imperialism and dictatorship in central America from the 1980s, taking the claims of the psychologists to discover and represent public opinion seriously and turning it against power (e.g. Martin-Baró 1994). The approach infused public opinion with humanist

values and notions of community consciousness-raising and active citizenship.

2   *English empiricism* re-emerged in studies of discrimination and inter-group conflict against apartheid psychology in South Africa from the 1970s, insisting that there were real observable and regular patterns of oppression (e.g. Foster and Louw-Potgieter 1991). Researchers in this tradition refused the phenomenological approaches that simply ratified the distinct life-worlds of different 'races' in favour of challenging and changing group identities.

3   *Black psychology* developed as an alternative to mainstream white-dominated psychology in the USA from the 1960s, adapting a range of qualitative and quantitative approaches from the mainstream (e.g. Howitt and Owusu-Bempah 1994). This approach turned the pragmatism of white psychology against the mainstream to affirm the identity of an oppressed group, taking up useful images of mental health and reclaiming them.

4   *Activity theory* arose out of behaviourist conditioning studies in the Soviet Union from the 1920s, linking psychology with cultural processes and turning away from a focus on the individual to the study of sign systems and joint zones of development, in which people go beyond what they believe they can do (e.g. Newman and Holzman 1993). These 'zones of proximal development' made change a crucial part of the research.

This international context for the development of varieties of psychological culture and investigation may also help us to avoid seizing on any one alternative system as an 'example' that can be transplanted from one place to another in the hope that it will thereby solve the particular problems we face with our own psychologies at home.

Subjects and experts, and the process of discovery

One way of enabling new knowledge to emerge so that we also make the process of obtaining that knowledge different from mainstream psychology is to treat our 'subjects' as experts on their own lives. To do this we need to be mindful of two things.

The first is that the ability to formulate exactly what that expertise is should not be taken for granted. After all, our expertise as psychologists does not lie in our ability to recite all the volumes of knowledge that we have read over the years, but rather in our knowledge of where to look for information when we need it. The display of 'knowledge' as evidence of expertise can even be a sign that the person concerned is very *unsure* about their expertise. The second is that display of expertise is always limited and given to others in specific contexts, and so research needs to attend to the context in which the knowledge is produced, and the relationship between the researcher and researched.

We know from anarchist studies of the development of science that it has only been possible to take things forward when scientists challenge taken-for-granted assumptions, when there is an ethos of 'anything goes' (Feyerabend 1975), and feminist work has shown how crucial the role of subjectivity and the relationship between 'experts' and the world is to good scientific inquiry (Morawski 1997). Radical research in psychology often opts for qualitative methods, but this is only because this is currently the site for the most advanced debates about the nature of scientific (and unscientific) research.

Box 1.3 *For and against 'quantitative research'*

Qualitative research in psychology has pitted itself against mainstream quantitative approaches that have dominated the discipline in the English-speaking world. This is not because quantification is wrong as such, but because psychologists often do quantitative research so badly. Two collections by members of the Radical Statistics Group provide an antidote to this mystification (Irvine *et al.* 1979; Dorling and Simpson 1999), and some suggestions as to how this problem might be tackled. Here are four ideas.

1 *Statistical knowledge* is of existing regularities, of patterns that are open to reinterpretation and change. This means that if we take statistics seriously it is not possible to use those descriptions to make any claims about universal fixed qualities of human behaviour or experience.

2 *Mathematical theories* of representation that underpin statistics are themselves the product of certain sets of social circumstances and political agendas. The idea of a 'normal distribution', for example, already contains certain assumptions about nature and the allocation and distribution of qualities.

3 *Statistics* provide representations of the world that reflect the material that has been identified and measured, and this material is already infused with choices made by the investigator. Choice of 'categories' specified in a correlation, for example, reflects assumptions about the way the world should be divided up.

4 *Statistical expertise* can be distributed so that particular techniques are available to those who can then make use of them in an

immediate way. The model of 'barefoot statisticians' working rather like local-level 'barefoot doctors' in China who know specific skills and who to ask for other skills, for example, can be used to make the knowledge more transparent to those that it affects.

Radical research can be quantitative, but the methodological questions about standpoint, knowledge, subjectivity and history are as relevant to statistics and other quantitative approaches as they are for the qualitative study of action and experience in psychology.

Accounting and evaluating in a contested network

Because quantitative psychologists have often been so sure and strident in telling people how they behave and think, it is tempting for qualitative psychologists to shrink back and refuse to say anything at all that will be contentious. This is the worst and most useless logical endpoint of the role of the researcher and rests on well-intentioned but mistaken attempts to reduce the research relationship to empathy and respect.

Against this, the most interesting research writing is that which presents an *argument*, a *polemical position* that is willing to open itself to disagreement. One of the characteristics of qualitative research is that the interpretation of material – whether of ethnographic diary data, interview transcripts, stories gathered of someone's life, spoken or written texts or material from the media gathered for psychoanalytic purposes – cannot be proved to be wrong simply if another plausible interpretation can be given in its place. The question is not whether a particular argument is correct or incorrect, but whether it is a plausible argument that makes sense in relation to the material and the chosen theoretical framework.

A further crucial aspect of research writing in qualitative research concerns the way in which the argument is made accountable to an audience. Usually in quantitative psychological research it is silently assumed that the research is worth doing if it will be read by an audience of fellow psychologists as part of the broader enterprise of accumulating scientific knowledge. And if the only audience for a piece of research is fellow psychologists, then the question of 'criteria' in the evaluation of the research then also tends to be too quickly defined and fixed before it has even been considered and thought through. Qualitative research that aims to make a difference in the very process of doing the work, if not in the consequences of it for others who are invited to read and puzzle and disagree with it, is the kind of research that raises the question from the beginning 'by what criteria should I be judged?' (This is a question addressed in detail in Chapter 10.)

Box 1.4 *The next steps: five methodological routes to radical research*

The separation of methodology into distinct approaches is convenient – too convenient and sometimes very problematic. Each approach contains within it assumptions about experience, language and reality that can lead the researcher away from the questions they really wanted to address. These five approaches are useful, but need to be used in a way that also makes them subject to question.

1 *Ethnography* – do you want to provide a coherent picture of the internal lived reality of a group, institution or community, or are you going to attend to the way different accounts reflect different interests?

2 *Interviewing* – are you going to try to respect the account given by someone whatever they say, or are you going to make your disagreement with what they say clear to them in the process of doing the research?

3 *Narrative* – will you assume that the story you piece together must really have a beginning, middle and an end, or are you open to be surprised by forms of narrative that break from this?

4 *Discourse* – are you going to confine yourself to what appears in a transcript or other kinds of text, or are you going to draw upon other material to make sense of what appears there?

5 *Psychoanalysis* – will you search for underlying psychological reasons to explain what is happening, or will you ask what is so compelling about the idea that there are underlying reasons in the first place?

We will follow through these questions in more detail in the chapters devoted to these approaches. The best research does not allow itself to be defined by its methodology alone, and innovation often proceeds by asking searching questions of one approach from the vantage point of the others, driven by the explicit and implicit political projects of the researcher.

We can only open the space for radical research in psychology using qualitative methods if the political stakes in each specific project are thought through, and this requires a willingness to search beyond the discipline for appropriate theoretical resources (Parker 1999a). This means drawing on work in other sites, perhaps in other 'cultures', where psychology is done differently in order to throw our own assumptions into question (e.g. Terre Blanche and Durrheim 1999). This may then help us to question our own understanding of what 'culture' is and how 'we' arrive at a sense of who we are in relation to those 'others' we study (Burman forthcoming). It means learning from other disciplines where debates in qualitative methodology have been able to go down quite different tracks because there are views of human action and experience that start outside the framework of methodological assumptions that characterize Anglo-US psychology (e.g. Denzin and Lincoln 2000). And it means developing a relation to other contexts of inquiry that draw attention to the limits of framing qualitative research in academic terms, forcing the question as to why a particular piece of work might be worth doing. This enables us to take each of the methodological frameworks discussed in this book closer to action research. Academic research groups may be one supportive resource for thinking through these issues, but they too will also be part of the problem if they turn innovative work into a new orthodoxy.

Further reading

Harding, S. (ed.) (1987) *Feminism and Methodology: Social Science Issues.* Bloomington, IN: Indiana University Press.

Parker, I. (2003) Discursive resources in the Discourse Unit, *Discourse Analysis Online*, 1(1): http://www.shu.ac.uk/daol/articles/v1/n1/a2/parker 2002001. html (accessed 29 October 2003).

Terre Blanche, M. and Durrheim, K. (eds) (1999) *Research in Practice: Applied Methods for the Social Sciences.* Cape Town: UCT Press.

2   Ethics

The ethical dimension of qualitative work emerges in political practice which bridges the gap between anticipation and reflection.

Arguments in social psychology for a 'new paradigm' during the 1970s often made the case that research was a 'moral-political' activity, that each stage in the research – choices we make about what to study, the way we go about the business of striking up relationships with participants, what we do with what we have found – has a moral and political dimension (e.g. Harré 1979). The connection between the moral aspect and the political aspect of the research – marked in the well-worn phrase 'moral-political' – drew attention to the way that our everyday treatment of others is intimately linked to wider social forces. We are always participating in the activity of either reproducing the way the world is or transforming it (Bhaskar 1986). It is, of course, quite possible to engage in this activity unthinkingly – blithely unaware or simply uncaring – or deliberately, and it is that careful deliberate thinking through of what might happen in our research, and reflection on what did happen, that may enable our research to be genuinely radical.

This does not mean, however, that we can ensure that we really are engaging in good moral-political research activity simply by being nice to people. Some of the people we study may have views about the world that are not only different from ours, but unpleasant and dangerous, and to collude with them or give them a platform would be, at best, unthinking sentimentality (Billig 1977). The 'political' side of the equation comes to the fore when we deliberately position ourselves in relation to those we are studying and those who may read our research reports, and when we are willing to take some responsibility for what we are doing. Radical qualitative research is psychological research that knows from the start why and how it participates in the world and then remains true to what happens there. This difficult contradictory world of 'political' relationships and their effects on others – political because the world is always being reproduced or transformed by our engagement with it – calls for a political assessment of the research from the beginning through to the end, something that feminist research has always recognized (e.g. Henwood *et al.* 1998). So the key question is how we stay true to what happened. This means that *fidelity to commitments made during a research event is the space for ethics*.

Most discussions of 'ethics' in psychological research, however, fail to follow through these moral-political issues (Prilleltensky 1994). Ethics is too often thought about mainly in relation to laboratory-experimental research, and morally questionable assumptions about the observation and measurement of the 'subjects' of the research are then counterbalanced by attempts to ensure that the 'subject' has the same level of self-esteem when they leave the study as when they entered it. Those discussions are useless at best or misleading at worst when they are applied to qualitative research. This chapter builds up an alternative case for ethics in research from entirely different premises.

Five resources for ethics

Basing an adequate account of ethics in psychology is a bad place to start, so we need to turn to contemporary debates well outside the discipline. The arguments in this chapter are based on the work of the French philosopher Alain Badiou (2001). For Badiou there are four ethical domains – science, art, love and politics – and in each of these domains there are three ways that evil arises. Psychological research is an enterprise that touches on each of the four ethical domains, when it tries to present itself as really 'scientific' or as an alternative creative artistic endeavour, and also when it explores the deepest human emotions of love and hate and finds itself all the while producing knowledge that has powerful political consequences. We can find a series of arguments – five resources – in Badiou's writing on ethics that can then be connected with qualitative research.

- First, we have to be careful not to start with assumptions about the nature of human beings that are either directly or indirectly derived from psychology. The discipline of psychology and popular commonsensical ideas about psychology that circulate around the discipline all too often lead us to think either that people are essentially good (and then we try and enable them to be good to us in the research) or deep-down bad (and then we are suspicious about everything they say to us). But *neither essential goodness nor badness lies inside human beings*. This means, for example, that psychology cannot divine any good news about human nature as part of or as an alternative to evolutionary models. The oscillation between descriptions of 'personality', which is assumed to be nice and healthy, and 'personality disorder' as something the discipline assumes to be psychopathic is an indication of how psychology fails to grasp the varieties of human 'nature' (see e.g. Parker *et al.* 1995). The question, instead, is how the good and the bad emerge and how they are judged.

- Second, we need to beware of the idea that the other people we encounter in research should be treated as if they are essentially the same as us. Psychology is usually happy to run with the idea that others are different, often all the better to pathologize them. Sometimes the discipline is happy to respect those differences, but usually then only on condition that those others are 'good others', that they do not do anything that might really disturb our ideas about what is normal and what is abnormal. Instead, it is better to go further and take as our starting point the idea that *others are not the same as us, and there is no reason why they should be.* Psychology should not be the basis for universal models of moral action which pathologize or wipe away differences between human beings. The lesson of the most radical research on different forms of identity is that we should not assume some underlying commonality between all psychological researchers and all those who are studied (Sampson 1993).

- Third, it is useful to work on the ethical basis that *respect of particularity is the route to transformation.* When we work on this basis we do not fall in line with the usual psychological practice of factoring in all the different aspects that are 'discovered' about a category of person into an overall scheme or model. Instead we notice the way that the grouping of descriptions always serves to screen out what is different, and in that way psychology obscures the way a system or model rests on patterns of exclusion and the production of 'others' with specific claims (see e.g. Phoenix 1994). It is then possible to take seriously what those particular differences reveal about what we take for granted and what we usually overlook.

- Fourth, we work on the basis that *the points of impossibility in research might reveal something important about the reality of the situation for participants.* That moment when we come up against a point of impossibility in a piece of research – the point where there is a contradiction between accounts or a discrepancy that we cannot make sense of – is not necessarily an 'error'. It is not necessarily the case that we have simply failed to gather enough information. Psychology should not search for ways to fit things together as if that is the way to truth. Instead it may be that the differences of viewpoint between the different participants (or between the participants and ourselves) are a function of such radically different lived realities and conflicts of political perspective that it would actually be a mistake to try and smooth over those differences using one overall covering account. The position of the researcher is not a clear 'standpoint' which gives one clear view of things to be compared with the others, and the fixing of an explanation from any particular standpoint can be a way of covering things over (Harding 1987).

- The fifth resource is the argument that *communities are not homogeneous*, an argument that also applies to any particular category of identity that is being studied. (The consequences of this point are examined in more detail in Chapter 4.) Psychology should not try to calculate the costs and benefits of certain courses of action for those in any group so that it can then balance out a judgement to arrive at some kind spurious 'equality' between the different sides. Psychological properties are not necessarily distributed among people and they are not held in common (see e.g. Harré 1984). Instead, it is more helpful to focus on the moments when members of a community or identity category challenge and refuse the attempt by others to make them fit into it. It is at those moments that we are able to see how the category functions to hold together a certain view of the world and, perhaps, to cover over and obscure real structures of exploitation and oppression.

Now let us move on to put these resources to work on the ethical issues that arise in the course of qualitative research.

Anonymity as alibi

Instead of focusing either on anticipation of things that might happen or reflection on what we have done, the account of ethics outlined so far emphasizes the importance of the practice which links anticipation and reflection. In this view truth depends on its own production, emerging in the *process* by which we discover something. Truth is intimately bound up with the conditions in which the knowledge is produced and the position from which the researcher is examining the phenomenon in question. This means that psychology should not try, as it usually does, to discover a truth for others independent of the particularities of a situation.

This crucial argument from Badiou's (2001) writing on ethics brings together the five resources – on the *construction* of good and evil rather than the attempt to discover it in human nature, on the attention to differences between ourselves and others we study, on our respect for the particularity of strange new perspectives as a new window on our taken-for-granted reality, on the points of impossibility in research as showing the structural limits of knowledge as an effect of structural differences of position, and on the essential heterogeneity of communities or categories of identity that we may be studying. Empirical truth is always constructed from a certain position. It depends on the actual process of production rather than something mysterious outside us, and so research has to reinvent the possibility for this truth to appear as something specific and surprising (Badiou 2002). Some new truth appearing in a specific and surprising way is one of the highpoints of good qualitative research. But what are the consequences here for 'ethical questions' in psychology, for the usual procedures for trying to ensure confidentiality and anonymity in research?

There is actually no such thing as 'confidential' research because the aim of the work is always to 'discover' something new and to show it to others. There is 'anonymity' in research, but rather than take this anonymity for granted as a solution to ethical problems – as to how we might protect our participants – it is better to treat anonymity as an ethical *question*. This question is something that can be turned towards our participants and then back to ourselves us as researchers.

For example, to conceal the identity of research participants might be the most convenient and easiest option, but not actually the most ethical one. One of the effects of the attempt to conceal a participant's identity is that they are thereby denied the very voice in the research that might originally have been claimed as its aim. It confirms one of the prevalent images of those who are researched by psychologists as fragile beings needing to be protected by others (K. McLaughlin 2003). This portrayal of people is itself an ethical position, one that subscribes to a therapeutic and humanist vision of what people are able to do and how they are able to change. The image obscures the resilience of human beings and makes it more difficult for the researcher to appreciate and support acts of resistance. It may be better to discuss openly with those who take part in research whether or not they might actually prefer to be named and to speak openly for themselves.

On the other side, the concealment and protection of the identities of research participants may operate all the more efficiently to seal off the researcher from those they study, actually serving to protect the researcher. And the demand by participants that they be identified might open the researcher to some discomfort, for it makes it easier for them to challenge interpretations that have been made in a report. So, the discussion with the participants about the value to them of anonymity may also draw attention to the stakes and privileges the researcher has in being able to control and disseminate information about the study (Lather 1995). The things that are 'discovered' in research are also always a *construction* of part of the world, and the researcher has a responsibility to make clear their own part in that construction so that the reader is in a better position to assess how and why they should take it seriously and even take it further. That position of the researcher is always, for good or ill, an ethical position.

Box 2.1   *A problematic starting point: the ethics committee*

Research proposals increasingly have to pass through one or more 'ethics committees', and while the process can be thought-provoking and sometimes useful, the ethics committee in a psychology department, hospital or local authority is often a nuisance that seems dedicated to putting obstacles in the way of the research. Radical qualitative research can be especially vulnerable when the committee operates on the assumption that people will do the worst unless they are prevented from doing so, and the peculiar institutional dynamics of the process means that 'ethical codes are by definition unethical' (Loewenthal 2004: 123). There are four reasons why you should not start with the ethics committee.

1   *Quantitative* – an ethics committee reproduces in its very functioning assumptions about quantification and measurement, and so the surprising things that happen in good qualitative research are treated with suspicion.

2   *Normative* – the committee tries to predict and control all the possible outcomes its members are able to anticipate, and so it then always tries to prevent new forms of research that fall outside these predictions.

3   *Bureaucratic* – the curse of the ethics committee is most evident in the 'checklists' that are endlessly expanded to cover every kind of research, and that always fail to capture exactly what it is you want to do.

4   *Routine* – the purpose of the committee is to make those who apply to it adhere to its rules, and the end result is usually to ensure dull conformity to get through the process and an end to serious creative thinking, an end to ethics.

Instead of taking the ethics committee as your starting point – or forgetting about ethics when you have finished with it – you should treat the committee as one specific audience for whom one kind of account is given of the research. You can play their game and risk corrupting your research or, better, you can think through the rules of the game so that your ethical decisions and fidelity to the research are deeper and even more wide-ranging than they would be able to imagine.

Transparency as theory

The role of theory in the production of apparently transparent research description connects with long-standing ethical debates in philosophy.

One example is the distinction between means and ends, and the debate as to whether it is right to do things that are in themselves morally objectionable (the means) in order to bring about some future good (the ends). Psychology has traditionally opted for the position that a little deception now and then will in the long run produce beneficial results. This version of ethics takes for granted that we must rationally anticipate what is going to happen and reflect on what we have done. Radical qualitative research outlined in this book, on the other hand, focuses on the way that the means that we adopt – kinds of question, relationships with participants, and forms of writing – will themselves give rise to certain kinds of effects. Ethics is now seen as a *practice* which bridges the gap between anticipation and reflection (and between means and ends). In this sense our qualitative research can be ethical right through the research. Although we may not believe that anything could be perfectly transparent – that we need some theory to make things understandable – we do aim to be accessible to those we work with and to those we want to persuade of the value of our work.

Badiou's (2001) work on ethics reminds us once again that theory in psychology need not be an obstacle to understanding the world, but is actually the very precondition for being able to make sense of what is going on. Against the commonsensical argument that we can only make the world transparent to the researcher by wiping away all our preconceptions, we come to see that an attempt to open a 'transparent' window onto the world requires a good deal of theoretical work. That theoretical work is part of the practice of good research.

Box 2.2   *Contexts for specifying 'ethics'*

Traditional accounts of ethics rest on certain assumptions about what is 'good', but there are some problems with each of the main paradigms. Traditional psychology fits very well with these paradigms, and so there is all the more reason to be careful about taking on board their assumptions about the 'good' (Parker forthcoming). There are three main paradigms that are historically derived from influential western philosophical frameworks for making sense of human experience and behaviour.

1   *Aristotle* assumes we can all agree what a 'good' is that we should be aiming at and against which we can easily define what falls below the ideal standard. In psychology, specifications of essential underlying human nature, perhaps deriving from the secular humanist tradition, for example, would presume that we do know what it is to do right and wrong. A problem with this paradigm is that what may be good for us as an ideal is suffused with irrational hopes and fears, and may then turn out to be quite horrific to other people.

2   *Kant* assumes that there is an imperative to follow the right course of action, which is potentially if not actually present in each individual human being. Psychological models of the person fit this paradigm, when they presume that the individual contains a conscience by virtue of which they are able to participate in society as a civilized and enlightened human being. The problem with this paradigm is that some people who carry out the most horrific actions feel themselves to be following some version of a moral injunction and to be in conformity with what human nature is like.

3   *Bentham* assumes that we should calculate the costs and benefits of actions for different individuals, and that it is possible to determine the way the greatest possible good could be distributed among them. Behaviourist psychology, which rests on notions of what healthy and unhealthy patterns of behaviour are and how contingencies of reinforcement might be set up to bring benefit to people, would fit with this paradigm. The problem is that some neutral position outside the system is presupposed so that decisions can be made by someone who is not themselves implicated in the system they have devised.

An account of ethics always contains within it a certain view of what a human being is – and what its 'psychology' is like – and so it is all the more important that radical qualitative research takes ethics seriously and finds a way of being all the more faithful to an alternative conception of ethics.

Representation as position statement

Qualitative research has been one of the driving forces in psychology, questioning the language that we use to describe those we do research with. Feminist researchers, who have been at the forefront of some of the most radical developments in qualitative work, have drawn attention to three aspects of the language we use, aspects with an ethical dimension.

The first is to find alternative ways of referring to what we used to call 'subjects', and to accord them agency in the research as 'research participants' or as 'co-researchers'. Different terms are appropriate in different kinds of research, but a decision about terminology here always has consequences. The second aspect is in the terms of self-reference that the researcher uses, with one key marker of this self-reference in qualitative research being to write in the first person – to take responsibility for what one did and to position oneself by saying that 'I did this'. The third aspect of language is in the claims to represent the experience of others who are research participants or co-researchers (Wilkinson and Kitzinger 1996). How one represents 'others' of different sexualities and cultures, for example, is a question that cannot be answered with any simple formulae, but is one to be thought through, and if at all possible talked through, with those who participate in a study.

Box 2.3   *For and against good behaviour*

Unfortunately there is no perfect fully-formed alternative system of ethics that could replace the mistaken individualist models in traditional philosophy and mainstream quantitative psychology. And there are some risks and uncertainties in ethical research that can only be encountered as dilemmas to be worked through in practice.

1   *Moralizing?* Is there not always a risk of turning any account of ethics into a system of morality to which we subject others, so that those who do not agree with us are moralized at and treated as if they were inferior to us? Here is one reason, perhaps, why a researcher might only want to consider the political consequences of their work.

2   *Rebelling?* Is there not always a risk in the challenge to traditional ethics, that the attempts by well-intentioned psychologists to prevent harm being done to others will be thrown out along with their mistaken models of what ethics actually is? Here is one reason, perhaps, why it might be worth participating in the ethics committees to make them open to new debates.

3   *Mistaking?* Is there not always a risk that the wrong decision might be made as to what the key 'events' in the research were and why we should remain faithful to them? Here is one reason, perhaps, why more meetings with colleagues about the ethics of the research rather than less might be a good idea.

The only thing we can be sure of is that in order to be ethical in our research we have to be badly behaved toward the discipline of psychology, but in such a way that is open to reflection; fidelity that is characterized by enthusiastic self-questioning rather than fanatical certainty (Hoens and Pluth 2004). The question is how we maintain some fidelity and good faith with more radical political projects for the transformation of human action and experience outside (and, if necessary, against) the discipline.

Institutional requirements as ethical frames

It is not possible to avoid the way one is positioned as a researcher, for the structural conditions of possibility for a piece of research to be carried out also impose sets of obligations – that one must follow certain procedures and that one will report on what one has done – and the institution within which we work also sends out powerful messages, that we are 'experts' or 'students' or that we have some kind of specialist knowledge or access to resources.

A certain degree of calculation is necessary to be able to frame the research for funding bodies or supervisors or research degree committees or ethical committees, and I cannot tell you here exactly how to deal with these different bodies. They are often idiosyncratic in their demands, and they may like to be deliberately vague about what the requirements are because they believe that only in that way will you think for yourself. You need to be able to assess what each of these different components of the institution wants so that it is possible to be able to keep open some space for your research to give rise to something that could not be predicted and controlled. Then the reflection on what the consequences were of the decisions you made is also part of the practice itself, rather than being disconnected from it and dealt with by ticking a form from the ethics committee. This position calls on you to remain steadfast with respect to the ethical commitments you make to the research and especially to those who agree to work on it with you. This does not mean that you cannot be sceptical about what people say, but that you should be clear about the terms on which you will make criticisms and suggestions; working within an agreed framework is then reflexively relational 'immanent critique'. (This argument is taken up in more detail in Chapter 3.)

Box 2.4   *The next steps: five methodological routes to ethical research*

There is no single set of guidelines for the ethical conduct of research that could be applicable to all forms of qualitative research. Rather, these are issues from the alternative account of ethics outlined in this chapter for the different kinds of radical qualitative research discussed in the rest of the book.

1   *Ethnography* – there are particular questions about the way the ethnographic researcher makes sense of their own position in relation to the 'points of impossibility' in a 'community' so that they are aware of who they might be siding with when they try to describe what is going on.

2   *Interviewing* – there are particular questions for the interview researcher who is willing to make the interview encounter into a

space for challenge, for contesting taken-for-granted assumptions rather than colluding with them so that 'immanent critique' is made possible throughout the course of the work.

3   *Narrative* – there are particular questions for the narrative researcher who wants to witness, explore and support the emergence of a narrative and who also, at the same time, wants to show how a form of narrative may be a function of certain sets of cultural-historical arrangements.

4   *Discourse* – there are particular questions for the discursive researcher who may be tempted to think that there are no 'ethical' issues because they are simply reading public texts, but who is willing to think about the way any and every interpretation will have effects on others who read the research.

5   *Psychoanalysis* – there are particular questions for the psychoanalytic researcher who is drawing on a hugely powerful interpretative apparatus to speculate about the material they are examining, and who also needs to think about how they should also throw that interpretative apparatus into question.

The best research – and all action research – starts with ethical considerations and follows them all the way through the work, and then through to the way the research is read and taken up by others.

This chapter has taken up aspects of Badiou's (2001) writing on ethics and elaborated them in relation to some of the moral-political questions we have to tackle in qualitative research, but there are deeper implications in his work for the way we think about the relationship between the discipline of psychology and evil. One only has to think of the history of psychological research into intelligence and racial differences to see how the ethical and political dimensions are intertwined and have had evil outcomes (e.g. Billig 1979). For Badiou, evil arises through 'simulacra' (fake copies of events which close things down, as when the ethics committee replaces the careful, thoughtful deliberation of the researcher with its own bureaucratic procedures), 'betrayal' (giving up and turning against what was opened up, as when the early ideals of the research are abandoned because they are too difficult and when awful reports are produced which normalize and pathologize behaviour in line with the worst of traditional psychology) and 'absolutization' (enforcement of an overall scheme to force agreement, as when interpretations are made which pretend to apply to all those involved in the research and which are extrapolated to all the others who are assumed to be like them). Badiou's work provides a more radical way of thinking through ethics in psychology (Parker forthcoming), one which also calls for a deeper attention to the role of reflexivity in research.

Further reading

Badiou, A. (2001) *Ethics: An Essay on the Understanding of Evil* (original published 1998, trans. P. Hallward). London: Verso.

Henwood, K., Griffin, C. and Phoenix, A. (eds) (1998) *Standpoints and Differences: Essays in the Practice of Feminist Psychology*. London: Sage.

Prilleltensky, I. (1994) *The Morals and Politics of Psychology: Psychological Discourse and the Status Quo*. Albany, NY: State University of New York Press.

3   Reflexivity

Reflexivity is a way of working with subjectivity in such a way that we are able to break out of the self-referential circle that characterizes most academic work.

Research rarely takes place outside academic, governmental or professional institutions, and all research is judged at some time or another against academic standards that emphasize objective knowledge over subjective truth. These academic standards usually treat objective knowledge as the only thing worth taking seriously, and the subjective aspect is assumed to be some kind of impediment that should be cleaned away before the report is delivered. At the same time, when the researcher is permitted to reflect on what they are doing it is often within taken-for-granted limits that are also set in place by academic institutions. The kinds of questions that are often asked have to be framed in ways that emphasize the individual, personal nature of what a researcher thinks and feels about the work. This background poses particular problems for reflexivity, especially when the researcher is engaged in anything approaching action research.

We need to find a way of locating ourselves within three layers of the academic context of research: historical assumptions we make about what research is and who should do it, institutional constraints on what questions can be asked and who can answer them, and personal alliances that open up some issues and close others down. Of the three layers, the institutional element is the key to radical research, and this element can only be given due weight through collective activity. This means that reflexivity is a way of *attending to the institutional location of historical and personal aspects of the research relationship.*

Subjectivity in research is very easy to caricature as the 'merely subjective' opinion of the researcher. Then it is something that carries no weight at all because it mistakenly makes its claim to be heard in contrast to the discovery of real hard facts in objective studies, or it relies on the goodwill of the reader to indulge the researcher so that they are willing to believe that something must be important because there is a strong plea that this or that is what the researcher really feels to be the case. Both are bad options. This 'merely subjective' version of subjectivity is misleading because it overlooks the difficult conceptual work that we need to engage in to make subjectivity part of the research, and it reduces subjectivity to something that only pertains to the individual researcher as if it were hidden inside them, waiting to be revealed to the reader (Parker 1999b). Against this, we need to draw on some theoretical frameworks to understand what subjectivity is, and to think of reflexivity as part of the collective activity that takes place in all research.

Three resources for reflexivity

These theoretical frameworks draw attention to the way our reflexive engagement in research can turn the 'merely subjective' into a self-consciously and deliberately-assumed position. This *position* of the researcher then makes subjectivity into a crucial resource in the research process, and into something that can be made visible to the reader so that it is also useful for them if they want to take the work forward.

- First, while a personal diary is a very useful resource – and some kind of record should be kept during the course of the research – memory is not something that is confined to the individual. In fact, we now know that much human memory is collective and relational in character (e.g. Middleton and Edwards 1991). One of the peculiarities of western psychology is that it assumes that cognitive processes happen in the head first and only then are shared with others. The revolutionary tradition of 'activity theory', on the other hand, drew attention to the importance of collective cognitive processes – with memory as one of the most striking instances – which *precede* and inform the way a particular individual thinks and remembers (e.g. Newman and Holzman 1993). The historical conditions of possibility for certain kinds of research questions to be asked, for example, are *collective processes*, not simply to do with whose bright ideas set a particular research agenda, and these processes are relayed through institutions (such as universities willing to fund the research and disciplines organized to pursue the studies). The lesson of this work is that the activity of a research team is crucial to the framing and interpretation of a piece of research and the research cannot be carried out outside a research relationship. The activity of the team may be implicit – present only in the meetings between researcher and supervisor – and the relationship with co-researchers conveniently overlooked, but these collective aspects of what is thought and what is remembered about the research process are crucial to reflexive work.

- Second, while our thoughts and feelings about what we do are important – and some space in the research diary for such reflection is useful – thinking and feeling impacts on others involved in the research through our embodied relation to them. It is this embodied relation that relays and reproduces so much of the taken-for-granted institutional privilege and power in research. Psychology usually focuses on power as something that is deliberately and intentionally wielded, but feminist studies of the *embodied relations* between men and women have shown that patterns of privilege are more complex than this. Studies have focused, for example, on features of language that routinely derogate the powerless, use of time so that those without power are the ones who wait, and control over space so that resources are dominated by certain groups (e.g. Henley 1979). There is clearly an issue here about gender in research, particularly in a discipline where most of the students are women and most of those who teach or lead research teams are men (Burman 1990), but this embodied relation between the powerful and powerless is also relevant to how an institution maintains structural positions so that certain people have access to expert language (which makes it seem like those who are studied are stupid), are able to set the timetable for the research (so that those who are studied must fit in), and have access to resources (so that the research takes place on their own ground). The way we move and carry ourselves through the institution and then relate to others by virtue of our position in the institution is also, then, a key question for reflexivity.

- Third, while we need to be able to take some distance from what we are studying – and a diary might be one way of creating space away from the immediate context of the research – this distance is still itself something that structures subjectivity. The tradition of research by Theodor Adorno and colleagues in the Institute of Social Research showed how every claim to objective truth is also simultaneously the reflection of the historically-embedded subjective position of the researcher in what they are studying (Buck-Morss 1977). There is a dialectical – contradictory and mutually implicative – relationship between researcher and researched, and this dialectical quality of all our knowledge about what we study means both reality and truth are always in themselves contradictory. What we find and the sense we make of it are always a function of what we thought we would find and the position we try to make sense of it from. Adorno argued for a particular form of inquiry – negative dialectics – which would operate as 'immanent criticism', searching out the contradictions in reality and turning the language that is used to describe something against itself to bring out the kernel of truth (Adorno 1973). This notion can be taken further in radical qualitative research so that a commitment can be made to the ethos of a project or with co-researchers, and then the interpretations that are made are from within a specific conceptual frame *and* sceptical, in and against dominant versions of reality. This *'reflexively relational immanent critique'* requires an attention to the role of subjectivity in research.

The process of collective remembering in research highlights the limits of bourgeois individualism (and not only this), an attention to the embodied relation of the researcher with those they study can make explicit gendered aspects of the research process (and not only this), and the development of immanent critique can operate within the framework of commitments to those inside and outside the institution so that reflexive questions can be asked about the location of the research and the academic terms of the knowledge that is to be produced.

Confessions (first person)

It is tempting to reduce reflexivity to an activity produced by someone speaking in the first person and with the activity then amounting to little more than a feeble confession about what has been done. 'I really believe this or that which is why I started the research', 'I felt this or that very powerfully while I was carrying out the research'; these kinds of first person account are the *beginning* of the reflexive work – maybe a necessary beginning and way into further analysis, perhaps useful material to be included in the personal research diary – but we should take care to ensure that they are not paraded as the last word on reflexivity.

One thing we learn from Adorno (1973) is that every attempt to be objective itself requires a particular form of subjectivity. Standard laboratory-experimental research, for example, requires the investigator to distance themselves from their objects of study, a move which not only dehumanizes the participants but also gives rise to a peculiarly robotic 'scientist' subjectivity, though still subjectivity nonetheless (Parker 1999b). The characteristic 'dialectical' move that Adorno's immanent critique of the opposition between subjectivity and objectivity allows us to make is to show that objectivity is deeply subjective, and that we may arrive closer to the truth, to an objective standpoint, by reflecting on our own subjectivity, on how we have come to be located in the research at this point in history in this particular institution. What we thereby bring to light is the 'unintentional truth' of our activity as we translate what Adorno termed the 'exact fantasy' we develop about what we are doing – something that has an intimate and necessary relation to the object of our study – into verbal or written form. This translation transforms the 'exact fantasy' into something public which is then made susceptible to further reflection (Buck-Morss 1977). This reflexive activity does not turn inward, to a simple first-person account confession, but outward to the social relations that have enabled someone to experience themselves as an individual in relation to others.

In this way reflexivity does not simply endorse a particular experience, making it the foundation for the claims that are made in the research, but questions that experience, asking how it might have come to be that I felt this or that about what happened (e.g. Walker 1988). That is, the self is not treated as the bedrock of experience but as something that is crystallized from historical and institutional structures. It is collective matter.

Box 3.1   *A problematic starting point: the self*

A striking feature of our existence as sentient beings is that our subjective sense of ourselves involves continual 'second-order monitoring' of our behaviour and cognitive processes (Harré and Secord 1972), but we do even this monitoring as a social practice (Burkitt 1991). Not only are we thinking all the time, but we spend a good deal of our time thinking about thinking. When we carry out that reflexive work we always either perform it explicitly with others, or it is implicitly collective. This is the case when, for example, we rehearse arguments we have had or will have with others, or are participating in collective activity through the process of using a language that we share with others. The self is thus a problematic starting point for thinking about reflexivity for five reasons.

1   *Culture* – the form of the 'self' varies from culture to culture, to such an extent that it does not make much sense to refer to it as being the same thing everywhere with identifiable universal characteristics.

2   *Locality* – the way individuals describe themselves even varies with respect to different social settings, so that it is difficult to assume underlying coherence as the touchstone of personal integrity.

3   *History* – the self as a thinking, feeling core of the human being seems to have emerged quite recently in human history, and so cannot be presupposed as essential and necessary.

4   *Temporality* – individual selves change quite quickly, adapting themselves moment to moment to different demands and stringing together those changes on the threads of memory.

5   *Self-identity* – the certainty of self-experience starts to unravel when we examine the way that our sense of ourselves is riddled with contradictions, to the point that even the 'identity' of the self cannot be taken for granted.

The 'self' is itself something socially constructed, but is able to weave for itself an illusion of coherence through its memory of relationships with others, and actual relationships which confirm its enduring existence for itself. Far from being a reduction to the level of individual subjectivity, reflexivity is a way of questioning the assumption that we should start with the individual 'self' as a taken-for-granted foundation for research. Or, maybe this means that we could start with the self as a tactic, and then reflexively locate it in the contradictory social relations in which we have had to carry out our research.

Positions (second person)

The experiences of the researcher can tell us something about what is going on, but only when those experiences are explored, so that we are led from the initial sense that some aspect of the research relationship was perhaps uncomfortable or disturbing in some way to then make something that was hidden or implicit more visible. Some of the most illuminating writing on this aspect of research has been from within the field of anti-racist and post-colonial research (Ashcroft *et al.* 1995). Instead of treating the 'other' culture as the only one marked by features of difference – difference from the assumed norm of the white researcher that lets 'our' culture off the hook – there is a painstaking attempt to 'colour in whiteness', to make visible the particular position from which the research is carried out ((charles) 1992). Writing within lesbian feminist research on the representation of others (e.g. Livia 1996), and autobiographical writing on the class nature of academic institutions (e.g. Walkerdine 1990) has also offered alternative ways of making visible what is usually overlooked in research.

Now the account is not simply a confession about what one feels, but an address to another and an attempt to explain to them how this subjective experience may have come about. The key point about this move from a first person to a second person account in the research is that we emphasize the *position of the researcher*. The position of the researcher is the structurally-constituted research subjectivity that has enabled some things to happen in the research and perhaps closed down other things. To talk about the 'position of the researcher' is not at all to wallow in one's own bad (or good) feelings about what happened in the research, to spill your guts about what you felt, but to explore how that particular form of subjectivity came to be the way it was by virtue of the particular institutional relationships that were drawn up and recreated and so to make it intelligible and accountable.

Box 3.2   *Contexts for describing where you are and what you can do*

Some of the most radical recent work on the way that psychology normalizes certain kinds of experience and pathologizes others has come from research elaborating a 'social model' of disability. The focus in this work has progressively shifted from those who do not fit because they suffer from a 'disability' – a variety of 'victim-blaming' – to how social practices exclude certain categories of people because those practices are 'disabling' (Goodley and Lawthom 2004). This social model of disabling practices has profound implications for other forms of oppression in academic, governmental and professional institutions, and so for the conditions under which research is carried out by academics on 'others' outside the institution.

1 *Gender* – aside from the domination of research institutions by men, traditional psychological research practice assumes stereotypically masculine features for predicting and controlling behaviour, formulating hypotheses from existing knowledge and then examining phenomena dispassionately. Not only are stereotypically feminine features devalued but alternative feminist perspectives on consciousness-raising, relational commitments and researcher standpoint are ruled out (Burman 1998a).

2 *Culture* – aside from the predominance of white researchers in mainstream institutions, traditional psychological research is carried out from within the perspective of the dominant culture, so that members of 'other' cultures are assumed to be the ones who have to be specified as different, marked out against the hidden normal behaviour and experience of the white population. The differentiation between what we take for granted and the category marked as 'other' also has consequences for how we define what research itself should look like (Phoenix 1987).

3 *Class* – aside from the gross under-representation of working-class people in higher education, the ethos of academic, governmental and professional research institutions prioritizes individual competitive activity, in which the bidding for resources privileges those who already have the time and the cultural capital (personal history, educational background, appropriate displays of self through accent, dress and leisure interests) to be able to accumulate even more resources and to sabotage collective forms of research with explicit political agendas (Walkerdine 1996).

It is an open question as to whether qualitative approaches will be able to challenge disabling practices in different institutions, and how radical research will be able to develop alternative ways of working against these and other dimensions of oppression. Reflexive exploration of the barriers to emancipation in research is at least a first step.

Theorizing (third person)

The position of the researcher becomes most evident, and also becomes easier to reflect upon, when it is explicitly treated as part of a *collective* process. Here, the necessarily relational character of human subjectivity is taken seriously, and the relational character of research is topicalized; that is, instead of simply treating it as a resource and then pretending that it is optional, we treat it as a topic, as an invaluable and essential aspect of research. It could be argued that this collective quality of the research – the fact that no research can be undertaken without the existence of other human beings and, in most cases, without their cooperation – is also testimony to the progressive potential of self-consciously 'proletarian' revolutionary research, research that aims not only to understand the world but also to change it (Marx 1845).

Some of the most innovative forms of research that bring this collective dimension into psychology have taken place within a framework that is both feminist and socialist, in the work of the German researcher Frigga Haug (1987). Haug's 'memory-work' – which is also closely related to the proposals by Adorno concerning 'immanent criticism', the bringing to light of 'unintentional truth' and the translation into verbal or written form of 'exact fantasy' – homes in on the knowledge that people already have about what they do and finds a way of rendering the knowledge into something true for them. With respect to the women she works with in her memory-work groups, for example, she argues that 'As experts on their own experience the individual women are both "producers of ideology" and the only ones who "know" how they did it' (Haug 2000: 156). A key methodological aspect of memory-work is that the accounts are rendered into the third person, so that the writer is able to create some distance from what they have experienced and thereby is able to reflect – *collectively* to reflect with others in the memory-work group – on how that form of subjectivity may have come about (e.g. Gillies *et al.* 2004).

This kind of research sometimes seems to entail the view that there is a 'collective subjectivity' to be accessed by participants (Stephenson 2003), but despite some theoretical problems, the approach opens up one way of bringing 'experience' into the equation without reducing that experience to something ineffable, dredged up from inside the self (Burman 2003).

Box 3.3   *For and against knowing your 'standpoint'*

The idea that 'standpoint' is the best way to make clear the position of the researcher (e.g. Hartsock 1987) has been challenged. One 'Marxist' challenge argues that you do not even need to know what the position of the researcher is in order to do radical research (Gegenstandpunkt 2003). There are at least three elements to the challenge.

1   *Reason* – the recourse to 'standpoint' leads to the substitution of a clear logic of argumentation by emotional appeals on the part of individuals to things they believe that cannot be validated or publicly and collectively reasoned about.

2   *Explanation* – the attention to 'standpoint' leads the researcher to explain away the conclusions of their research, tracing every claim that they make to other reasons why they have come to think the way that they do.

3   *Politics* – the feminist 'standpoint' theorist turns the argument that the personal is political into the assumption that the only things worth talking about are personal ones.

These objections to 'standpoint' also, of course, lead to a refusal of reflexivity as such, and standpoint theorists could easily reply that, for these criticisms, in the place of reflexivity all we are left with is a pretence to objectivity that will only work if there is a leap of faith, a subjective leap into a peculiarly dogmatic position.

Crafting (fourth dimension)

An account must be produced about what has been done, and this institutional demand for some kind of report is the only thing that a qualitative researcher can be sure about. (I deal with the writing of the report in some detail in Chapter 11.) But the way this account is crafted poses some important questions for the way the subjectivity of the researcher is made explicit in the research. Reflexive analysis should not make the claim that anything that happened in the research was 'spontaneous', for the question should always be directed at what the conditions were that could have made this or that unexpected thing happen. The claim that the relationships in the research were open and free-flowing with no limits should also be avoided, for this kind of claim is usually the most efficient way of covering over disagreement and power relations between researchers and researched (Freeman 1996). And when there are disagreements between the researcher and those they have worked with, we need to explore how these disagreements are to be voiced as part of an immanent critique of taken-for-granted assumptions.

The key reflexive question to be asked here is whether or not the interpretations that are being elaborated in the report lie within the terms of the commitment that was made to the co-researchers. The commitment itself varies according to the kind of research that is being carried out, and according to what kind of explicit alliance was made with those who took part, of course. In some cases, for instance, the researcher may have no sympathy at all with those they research, and so the grounds of the commitment that is made to them may be strictly circumscribed by another kind of commitment (to those who suffer at the hands of those who take part, or those who would suffer directly or indirectly by their views being given a platform). Different forms of qualitative research and distinct projects demand different levels of experiential link with co-researchers, different expectations that a researcher will be sympathetic and supportive, and different opportunities for the researcher to challenge what they find.

Box 3.4   *The next steps: five methodological routes to reflexive research*

Each form of qualitative method opens up different spaces for subjectivity to be thought about and talked about. The task in radical research is how to develop reflexivity appropriate to the different methods *and* to reflect on the limits of their different assumptions about the role of reflexivity.

1   *Ethnography* – in what ways are you an outsider who wants to get inside a particular community, or an insider who wants to be able to get some distance from it, and how are you positioned on one side or other of the boundary between inside and outside?

2   *Interviewing* – to what extent do you intend to disagree with those you are interviewing, perhaps even making explicit that disagreement, or intend to empathize with them, to recognize and validate what they say, perhaps so that you are led to some disturbing conclusions about what you believe?

3   *Narrative* – are you hoping for a clear beginning, middle and end of your journey through the research, so that your narrative mirrors the narrative of the co-researchers, or are you prepared to look at what does not fit, at what would be covered over if you were to smooth out your journey and theirs?

4   *Discourse* – what role are you going to accord to your membership of a culture, and how are you going to make those cultural resources outside the text explicitly into something to be drawn upon in the reading, but also stepping back and noticing things you take for granted?

5   *Psychoanalysis* – to what extent are you going to make use of your ambivalence toward the material, making your own investment in a certain kind of interpretation explicit, and how then are you going to find a way of talking about this that is also sceptical about psychoanalysis?

The underlying question – a collectively reflexive question – that needs to be thought through each time, with those who take part in the research and those who are explicitly or implicitly part of the research team, is *how reflexive issues may need to be reframed by different qualitative (and quantitative) methods.*

You will have noticed in this chapter that you are not being told simply to think very hard, as if strenuous cognitive activity will do the reflexive work we need in qualitative research. You are not being asked to delve into deep buried emotions, to tell us all about the things you feel as you do the work, for that will not really help the reader know more about what is going on. Still less are you expected to confess secrets about your own background; that might be an interesting therapeutic exercise for yourself, but it really is of little interest to someone trying to make use of your research (Davies 2000). It could be the case that an account of your 'personal journey' through the research process would illuminate the report, but only if that journey is used as a narrative device to draw attention to the way certain aspects of the research have been highlighted and other aspects left by the wayside (Finlay and Gough 2003). Reflexivity should not be a self-indulgent and reductive exercise that psychologizes phenomena and psychologizes your own part in producing them. Instead, the reflexive work is part of the action, and in action research much of that reflexive work is undertaken alongside and in collaboration with co-researchers (and then they have some reflexive work to do with you as well). The next chapters on particular methods in qualitative research show how reflexivity can, instead, be part of a radical questioning of psychology itself.

Further reading

Haug, F. (ed.) (1987) *Female Sexualization*. London: Verso.

Newman, F. and Holzman, L. (1997) *The End of Knowing: A New Developmental Way of Learning*. London: Routledge.

Walkerdine, V. (1990) *Schoolgirl Fictions*. London: Verso.

4 Ethnography

Ethnography can enable us to describe the self-representations a 'community' assumes and refuses in its relations with others.

Ethnography is sometimes characterized as the fairly innocent practice of 'hanging around' an organization or community and 'making something of it' (e.g. Bowers 1996). However, the history of ethnography is a history of observation, interference and control, intertwined with the history of colonialism; for the ruling of others was much more efficient when it was possible to understand better local 'native' perceptions of the colonizing power (Clifford and Marcus 1986). As important as the explicit colonial relations between the observers and those they want to study are, internal power relations also hold an oppressed community in place. Colonial power tended to cultivate a layer of obedient servants who would be granted special privileges and would be encouraged to think they were better than the rest of their community, perhaps even coming to believe that they were nearly as worthy as those who controlled them (Cooke and Kothari 2001). This is why some radical theoretical resources from anti-colonial struggle are relevant to contemporary ethnographic research (e.g. Fanon 1967, 1970).

Ethnography that calls upon the services of trustworthy 'informants', then, always risks encouraging those who have already sold out to sell the ethnographer stories about themselves that fit with the views of their world that they think are called for by the research. To be aware of this risk and to try to avoid it, then, we need to treat every representation of a community, whether it comes from the outside or the inside, with suspicion. The task is to show how a community fabricates images of itself in such a way as to conceal internal conflicts and to show how those conflicts may lead to the unravelling of the stories that make it seem that all is in order. It is in this light that *ethnography documents the invention and decomposition of communities*.

All good empirical psychological research is ethnography of one kind or another, and some of the most innovative studies in the discipline have included this methodology as part of the work (e.g. Rosenhan 1973). The question is what level of ethnographic description is produced. Even laboratory-experimental approaches would not be able to produce any 'data' if the researcher did not closely observe the behaviour of their 'subjects'. Quantification of observed behaviour tends to eradicate anything of interest, and it certainly obscures the meanings subjects attribute to their actions – and the attribution of meaning by the researcher is mediated by the coding of the behaviour (e.g. Buckle and Farrington 1994). Participant observation increases the involvement of the researcher in the phenomena, but all too often the positive impact of the participation is wiped out in psychological research when the material is reduced to numerical form. In this chapter we move well beyond 'observation' and 'participant observation' to radical ethnographic exploration of the life-world of a community and the contradictions that structure it. The researcher in this kind of work is always involved in some kind of 'action' even if they do not want to deliberately turn their research into action research.

Four key ideas in ethnography

Every description of a phenomenon is suffused with conceptual assumptions. These assumptions are views of the world which are either taken for granted, and so operate as hidden lines of force that bend the description in directions the researcher may not be consciously aware of, or are theoretically elaborated so the writer is able to make decisions about how they represent what they find and the reader is able to assess the value of the description. Four key ideas in ethnographic research – defamiliarization, power relations, impossibility and virtual space – help make the writing and reading of research open to this process of deciding and assessing, even if the ideas presented here will not ensure agreement over what is to be made of the description.

- First, although the researcher's initial encounters with a new life-world may be confusing, they need to beware of the transformation of the strangeness into familiarity. A community or subculture that they do not know will always very rapidly turn into something they think they know all too well, and so what is potentially interesting about the work starts to evaporate. The writing of a diary account through the course of the research should aim to keep alive the process of *defamiliarization* (cf. Bennett 1979), or making strange what the researcher finds. One way this can be achieved is by treating the things the members of a community say about it as aspects of 'self-presentation' (e.g. Goffman 1971), and the description of a subculture can in this way focus on how its members compose themselves in order to differentiate themselves from others (e.g. Hebdige 1979).

- Second, the researcher is liable not only to overlook what originally seemed strange to them as time goes on, but to start to take for granted what certain members of a community might tell them about how things are organized. As they get drawn into the particular language of a life-world they may lose sight of how that language is organized around patterns of *power*. It is worth keeping in mind that language always operates in the service of power, as feminist studies of the privilege given to men by the English language have shown (e.g. Spender 1980). Every dimension of oppression is reflected in and reproduced by language (Andersen 1988), and some of the classic ethnographic studies of the reproduction of class, for example, have focused on the way a subjugated group may find a way of resisting power, but with a cost: that they still end up with the kinds of 'career' that keep existing relations of power in place (e.g. Willis 1980).

- Third, the ethnographic researcher needs to know that a community will always circulate different representations of itself among its members. Although the contradictions between the different accounts may well be a function of the way the members are presenting themselves to an outsider – a crucial aspect of 'self-presentation' in research relationships (Marsh *et al.* 1974) – there will also be *points of impossibility* where there does not appear to be underlying consensus within the community. One of the most powerful descriptions of this point of antagonism in a culture was developed in social anthropology; disagreement between dominant and subordinate groups as to how a community was to be represented was crucial. There was even disagreement over how the disagreement should be represented, and the researcher had to conclude that this very disagreement structured the internal life-world of the community (Lévi-Strauss 1963). We might interpret differences of interpretation about the importance of 'class' as an explanation for social conflict in a society in this kind of way; those who benefit from the existing arrangements may not even believe that there is such a thing as class or that they are members of a dominant group (cf. Marcus 1986).

- Fourth, ethnographic work needs to focus on the different kinds of space that operate inside a community, and the way these spaces provide opportunities for resistance or escape, the way they may provide the *illusion* that there is resistance or escape (Hook and Vrdoljak 2002). Anthropological descriptions of new forms of 'non-place' in contemporary culture – spaces dedicated to transport, commerce or leisure – have shown how a place may negate the construction of collective identity or the possibility of resistance (Augé 1995). The emergence of new 'virtual' spaces in electronic networking – such as bulletin boards, chat rooms and email lists – have shown how new forms of resistance may be possible (e.g. Gordo López and Parker 1999). These different kinds of space pose new questions for ethnography (Hine 2000), and the task then is how to integrate exploration of these new 'virtual spaces' with an account of real-world relations of power and alternative forms of identity.

Qualitative research that uses ethnographic methodology can make explicit the way the different members of a little life-world represent themselves to their own 'community' and to the outside world, but always with a view to putting those performances into question – making them strange – and asking who benefits. This research does not try to smooth over the differences between the accounts but focuses on these differences – the points of impossibility – in order to show how power is exerted and what strategies are used by those who are trying to contest or avoid power. The task, then, is not simply to show the internal shape of one kind of space, but to show how many different contradictory spaces coexist in a community, and what we might learn from those contradictions as the community invents itself and tries to prevent itself from falling apart.

Box 4.1   *Beware community psychology*

If the main problem in psychology seems to be its methodological focus on the individual, then it would seem that a shift of focus to the 'community' would solve the problem. But it does not, because all of the old assumptions of individual psychology can very easily be raised up a level and adapted in order to define what a community is and how the psychologist thinks it should work. This means that the U.S 'community psychology' that emerged as a complement to mainstream psychology is not really an alternative all (cf. Prilleltensky and Nelson 2002). Ethnography working in this framework then becomes part of the problem rather than part of the solution. The problem is fourfold:

1 *A normalized image of what a community is or should be* means that the community psychologist idealizes what they think the community is that they are observing and working with. Because they think they know who really represents the community, they listen to certain people who are happy to talk to them and maintain the exclusion and oppression of those who do not.

2 *A pathologized image of those who do not fit in* means that the community psychologist thinks they can find out what is preventing the community from working smoothly. Because they

make alliances with certain representatives of the community they become part of an apparatus that will whip into line those who have refused to go along with the dominant community self-image.

3   *Enrolment of 'good citizens'* means that community psychologists not only have a view of what a good community is, but also a corresponding view of what a good citizen is who contributes to the community. Because the psychologist is so keen to involve everyone in their community they try to enrol everyone into active participation, so those who refuse are treated as spoilsports or worse.

4   *Control of the community to keep it sweet* means that the community psychologist works according to an agenda that is external to their target group. Because a governmental agency, funding body or research team has the 'community' as its object of study, a 'colonial relation' is set up with the community and there is recruitment of those inside the community who are willing to sell out.

'Community psychology', then, glues together the two terms 'community' and 'psychology' in such a way as to psychologize what a community is – to treat the community as something that can be conceptualized and studied by psychologists on their own terms – and then to use that psychologized image of the community to understand the individuals that comprise it. Many well-meaning community psychologists make exactly this mistake in a bizarre double move that betrays all of the good things they hope to do with a community. It would be possible to call this 'action research', but it is actually quite a conservative form of action, one that maintains power relations rather than challenges them. Some psychologists do not do this, but when they do not they have to abandon dominant images of psychology and community and find something better.

The next two sections focus on how ethnography can be put to work to explore the way a community invents itself and holds itself together and then how it attempts to regulate its members and prevent resistance.

Degrees of inclusion and separation

A community may intrigue the researcher, but idle curiosity is not a good enough reason to carry out ethnography. It may be useful to think about a piece of ethnographic work as having two parts; in the first part the researcher develops a commitment to the community in question and focuses on the 'invention' of the community; in the second part the researcher is more sceptical about every claim made by each participant and focuses on the 'decomposition' of the community. The two parts may be only hazily and imperfectly conceptualized at the outset, but it is with that division of labour between the two aspects of the research as the overall frame that we can now focus, first, on the 'invention' of the community to develop some research questions.

A first question may be a reflexive one for the researcher, about their investment in the community (an investment that may be only emotional but may also be more directly and immediately financial, that they already give resources or want to give some resources to those they intend to study): *what is my commitment to this community?* This question can then be elaborated in more detail as a research question that specifies what it is about the community that is worth examining. A second question concerns *how it may be possible to document what is happening.* And this question too requires some careful thinking through of what the 'position of the researcher' is, and whether it will be possible to discuss with the community that some ethnographic research is taking place. A third question concerns *the lessons that may be learnt from the description*, and this third question needs to be elaborated in such a way as to link the position of the researcher to the kind of description that can be written. For example, how are the grounds on which a critique might be made to be decided, how are the lessons to be developed, and is it to be in collaboration with the community?

An example community context for ethnographic work:

Rahila (the researcher) has started work in a community mental health organization, 'Care Practice', in a large city in the industrial heartlands of Britain. The organization was initially developed ten years previously by those involved in alternative mental health movements who were campaigning for patient rights against the traditional psychiatric models used in the wards of hospitals. It grew to its present size, with some 200 employees, after bidding against the state sector clinics and other private organizations to provide better services for patients in the community, and it now runs residential homes and a series of 'outreach' teams that support people who have been discharged from mental hospital. Many of those involved ten years ago are now senior managers in the organization. Rahila was specifically employed to help set up a new 'internet café' in one of the run-down areas on the edge of the city. She started her work with the organization before she began the ethnographic work, and so the first stages of the research involve some reconstruction through diaries and discussion with colleagues who have now left the organization of what it was that attracted her in the first place.

This description is written in the third person to enable Rahila to get some distance from the organization and her own role within it. (See the account of this strategy in 'memory-work' discussed in Chapter 3.) She will rewrite this little description every now and then, and this will help her track her changes in understanding what is going on, and her relationship to it. Her reconstruction of the first stages of her involvement with the organization enabled her to focus the research questions for the study. Her background includes some activity around alternative mental health work, and so she wants to make a difference, seeing Care Practice as a practical alternative to mainstream psychiatric provision. The process of documenting the community, however, is going to be difficult because she has been taken on as an employee, not as a researcher. She decides not to tell the managers that she is taking detailed notes about the organization, but she does plan to produce a report that could provide a public record of things that are working and things that are not working in Care Practice. In this sense, Rahila has hopes to produce a piece of work that is 'policy-oriented', and that work aims, as far as possible, to be constructive. It is the constructive aspect of the research that she will be able to focus upon most easily in the first part of the research, on the 'invention' of the community. The way she starts to go about this work can be described as taking place in three steps.

Rahila begins by reconstructing not only her own contact with the organization and the process by which she was appointed, but also how she came to learn about the history and political project of Care Practice (*Step 1*). What she knew about that history and politics already had some positive impact on her first impressions of the organization and the relationships she was able to make in the lead up to the interview. In this sense, she knows that she wants to engage in some form of 'reflexively relational immanent critique', and the common ground she explicitly shares with the founders and current management of the organization – respect for the rights of patients and commitment to alternative non-medical mental health provision – will be the basis on which she makes her report. That is, she takes their claim to adhere to these principles seriously, and it is by those principles that she will judge them. (See Chapter 3 for a discussion of immanent critique as a feature of the reflexive position of the researcher.)

The next step (*Step 2*) is to describe the culture of the organization in such a way as to draw attention to the different 'subcultures' within it. In the first few weeks of her time with Care Practice she heard some complaints from other workers about the management, and she makes notes on the different versions of the personal grudges that were being rehearsed to her as a newcomer. The question she asks herself here, as she is faced with members of the organization trying their best to present themselves to her in a good light, is what kind of alliances she is being drawn into, and what the consequences of those alliances will be for other participants in the organization who might want to speak to her or might be wary of speaking to her. The first three months (during which time she decides that she does want to carry out ethnographic research in the organization for a part-time research degree at a local college) are frustrating because the internet café has not actually been set up yet. This means that Rahila has no permanent base in the organization, but it also means that she has opportunities for easier access to different components of it. As she moves around, she documents the way different groups of workers try to cope with their dissatisfaction with the management and apparent uncertainties about the future of the organization.

The first two steps lay the groundwork for writing a report, but Rahila's notes so far are rather fragmentary, and all she seems to have assembled is a history of the transformation of a voluntary organization into a service provider and some scraps of gossip about former activists in management who have, she is told by others, 'sold out'. It is only when the internet café is actually set up and she is able to spend time there trying to do the job she was appointed to do that she starts to see some of the forces that are at work in the organization actually playing themselves out. When Rahila is able to make a connection between different groupings inside the organization – who speaks for the organization, and who must keep quiet about shortcomings – this leads her to focus on questions of power (*Step 3*). She notices how the 'ethos' of the organization is described differently by different groups, and this helps to solve a puzzle which has preoccupied her, which is that while the management are portrayed as 'authoritarian' and 'simply concerned with making money' they do not actually seem to be leading the organization in any particular direction at all.

Two different groups of workers emerge in Rahila's description. One group interprets the management as wanting the organization to run efficiently and compete with rival potential bidders for care services. The other group is reluctant to be involved in just another traditional psychiatric care organization and so they tend to avoid the decision-making bodies. Neither group experiences themselves as having power, but they each contribute to reinforcing the power of the management (a power that the management themselves do not seem to want to exercise). Now Rahila is torn between the two groups of workers, and it is this divided loyalty that she describes as part of her ethnographic study. Her initial commitment to the organization has now changed into a sense that she does not want to be allied to any particular subgroup. It is the specific way that the community has 'invented' itself as the continuation of the radical mental health movement that makes any disagreement or conflict liable to be interpreted as betrayal, and the impending competition for resources from mainstream service providers makes it all the more difficult to bring differences in the organization out into the open. In this way Rahila is able to deepen her understanding of some of the different alliances with power structures in the organization, and, just as importantly, the way the internal structure is manifest to outsiders.

Micropolitical features of power and space

Now we are able to move on to the second crucial part of the ethnographic work in which we focus on the 'decomposition' of the community. Here Rahila reflects on the commitment she has to Care Practice, and how she might document what is happening so that those involved might actually learn something from the process. Here she uses three 'micropolitical devices' to highlight how acts of resistance inside the organization are neutralized. But first she goes through her notes and, again using a third person form of writing to get some distance from the organization and her own role within it, she reformulates what the ethnographic research has come to be about:

> Rahila is working for Care Practice, and feels torn between the publicly-presented ethos of the organization (with which she agrees, and which was one of the reasons why she joined) and the different groups of workers (who have justifiable complaints about the bureaucratization of the organization, but who offer no constructive alternative). The internet café is one space in the organization that she feels comfortable in, and she is now focusing on the different networks of communication between the various dissident groups.

Rahila now focuses on control over information and the way the different 'subcultures' inside the organization set up their own networks as alternative sites of power.

First micropolitical device – find the points of conflict and attend to how these points of conflict are covered over. Rahila has already documented disagreement, but now she takes this part of the analysis further to explore how the conflicts are manifest to members of the organization. The internet café has been running for three months, but it is not attracting many customers. Although some users of mental health services who are already 'clients' of Care Practice are encouraged to use the place, 'outsiders' seem to have the impression that it is a private organization. The Care Practice logo on the window of the café seems to mark it out as some kind of local government social service organization. And the other clientele are Care Practice workers who drop in to talk to Rahila, to browse on the internet or to communicate with colleagues by email. Here Rahila is a victim of her own success as a researcher, for she is so willing to listen to different workers talk about their grievances that she has come to function as a particular kind of 'insider' herself; she has become known as someone who will give her time to people (and the workers make a contrast between this willingness to listen and the lack of concern shown toward them by their managers). It is only quite late on in the research that Rahila realizes that the internet café has actually become a key site for the covering over of conflict; by coming and using the computers (and talking to her), the workers have refuge from the jobs they find disappointing and dissatisfying.

Second micropolitical device – describe the fantasy spaces where people imagine they are free from the community. The internet café became a place where disaffected groups came in to sit around and complain about the management. Nothing else actually seemed to happen in the café, and the people just seemed to sit around as if they were not hurried and stressed, in the way they were in other parts of the organization. It was a kind of 'non-place', and an important aspect of this non-place was that it was somewhere the workers could access alternative networks of communication through email. As well as the internet, the email connections provided places where gossip could be exchanged, and Rahila was then able to note the way that email was used to provide strategies for countering the management. These included organizing alibis for meetings that were to be missed, arranging and covering up for 'sickies' (days off work due to ill health), and setting up work parties that would exclude certain people in the organization.

Third micropolitical device – show the contradictory features of the fantasy spaces. The spaces in a community that seem to provide points of escape (virtual or not) also often play a functional role for the community, and may not actually be so subversive. In this way the 'non-places' in the organization – the actual physical place of the internet café and the virtual places of email lists that people escaped into – used up labour time that should have been devoted to making the organization run more efficiently, but it also served to drain off energies that could have been channelled into challenging the management.

We have tracked changes in Rahila's position as researcher as a way of illuminating relations of power in the organization and the various actual and virtual spaces of resistance that exist within it. Rewriting the description of the research is a useful device for the researcher to highlight how their loyalties change during their time in a community, and how they ally themselves with different components of the organization when its members present themselves to the outside world. (The last stage of this particular ethnography – that appeared to be a footnote to the research but was eventually written into the report – was a description of Rahila's departure from the organization after the internet café was closed down because it was 'not financially viable'.) The three micropolitical devices – focusing on points of conflict and how they are covered over, on fantasy spaces as places of refuge, and on the contradictory features of those spaces – were ways of making networks of communication and patterns of power more explicit in the organization. In this case even more traditional qualitative research on virtual communication can be useful as an aspect of the research (e.g., Murray and Sixsmith 1998; Sixsmith and Murray 2001). It also connects with research on the way new technologies are used by those who have been powerless, developing new bases for power (Gordo López and Cleminson 2004). Box 4.2 mirrors these three micropolitical devices in ethnographic research, as the reverse bad image, with an account of the first stages that you should be careful *not* to follow in your research.

Box 4.2   *Stage by stage to ethnography*

These six stages are what you should not do, and they exemplify the bad practice of some ethnographic research.

1   *Wash your hands* – where you prepare yourself for this operation by making sure that you are completely cleansed of any material that might contaminate the community you are proposing to work on. A completely antiseptic start will guarantee your neutrality.

2   *Reassure your patient* – where you tell the community something about the procedure you intend to adopt, but be sure to minimize the dangers and, if necessary, get them to sign a waiver form (from the ethics committee) that ensures that you will not be held liable for any harm.

3   *Administer the anaesthetic* – where you make sure that the community knows nothing about what you are doing once you have opened it up. It is easier to conduct a thorough exploration of its insides if it is not conscious about your intervention and does not react unpredictably to the operation.

4   *Explore and extract* – where you find what is causing the problem and decide whether to deal with it there and then. A blockage might be dealt with by clearing it out or by installing a bypass. You will, at any rate, need to extract anything of interest and present it to an audience of your learned colleagues.

5   *Swab out and stitch up* – where you close up the point at which you entered and stitch over the wound as carefully as you can, with the aim of making it seem as if there had been no operation. Don't leave anything behind. Remember there is an important cosmetic aspect to this process, and the body should look nice when you leave it.

6   *Follow-up treatment* – where you may have to return to the conscious patient and give them some partial information that is designed to make them feel better, and to remind them that use of specialized language to describe them is the privilege of the experts.

The stages are presented here as warnings as opposed to prescriptions because ethnographic research requires intensive reflexive engagement with *problematic* aspects of a community rather than the bringing out of the good news that those in charge would like outsiders to hear.

Observing risks to the self in ethnographic research

An ethnographic piece of work poses particular questions about the ethics and politics of research. It is not usually possible, for example, to inform every member of a community that their little life-world is being closely observed and that what they say will be used to construct an image of the conflicts and contradictions that structure relationship networks (Clifford and Marcus 1986). In some cases it is possible to be quite open, and knowledge that those involved are taking part in an academic study will then form part of the research report (e.g. Willis 1980). However, some forms of ethnographic research could not be carried out if there was full open disclosure to all participants about the nature of the study.

The researcher may not be sympathetic to the communities under investigation, and their knowledge that they are being observed may make the research impossible. Some of the investigative journalism into the activities of 'cults', for example, could only be carried out by going under cover into different organizations (e.g. Shaw 1994). Investigative research into racist aspects of police authority subculture or that of immigration regulation services requires quite a high degree of deception.

The researcher may want to involve other co-researchers as part of a broader study of patterns of culture that include so many people that it is unfeasible to notify everyone that they are being observed. Some of the studies of British culture carried out by the 'Mass Observation' movement between the two world wars, for example, drew upon thousands of informants who made careful and detailed anthropological investigations of work and leisure (e.g. Madge and Harrison 1939). Studies of the ceremonies and superstitions of a culture and close examination of everyday practice call for some degree of discretion if they are to be successful.

The researcher may not initially know whether what they are involved in will be suitable material for ethnographic study, and it is just not sensible to notify participants in every strange situation that one starts to become acquainted with that they may at some point be described for academic purposes. It would in some cases make the level of familiarity that is necessary to produce a richly-textured account of patterns of meaning in a dominant culture – where the focus is precisely on racism, for example, or where the researcher is from a minority community – impossible (e.g. Bhavnani and Phoenix 1994). Everyday practices of sense-making are all, to some degree or another, 'ethnography', and it is when we start to frame them as such that the range of 'ethical' and 'risk' issues explicitly starts to come into play.

There is in every ethnographic study an ethical dimension that needs to be taken into account by the researcher, and this emerges in an assessment of the risks that are involved for them and for others. The proliferating committees concerned with 'risk' or health and safety in research are as irritating as those dedicated to 'ethics', but it is still worth reflecting on how the risks to be undertaken will impact on the position of the researcher, and what the costs will be in terms of the kind of knowledge that is produced, the extent to which it can be shared with others, and how it might benefit them.

Box 4.3   *Marking out the pitfalls in ethnographic research*

Things that should be avoided, and which would count against a good evaluation of an ethnographic report, include the following observations:

1   *'I was lucky to gain the community's trust and respect'* – this happens when you have been so anxious to be accepted that your object of study has either taken pity on you and decided to humour you, or certain layers in the community have made a calculated decision to ally with you. You need to always keep open the question of how you are perceived.

2   *'I witnessed things that outsiders rarely see'* – this happens when you imagine that the dramas of everyday life are not enacted for an audience. They always are, and there is no such thing as 'backstage', especially when a community knows that you are there to watch them. You need to always leave open the possibility that what was enacted was how they wanted to appear to others.

3   *'Everyone's voices have been included in this report'* – this happens when you have been lured into one of the most powerful guiding fictions of a community, that it includes everyone or that anyone worth talking to has been visible to you. You need to always leave open the possibility that there are other accounts, and to reflect on the divisions in a community that might have excluded them.

4   *'This is an account that they would be happy with'* – this happens either when you have persuaded yourself not to show the community the report (because you believe they would be happy with it) or when you have reflected an image of the community that fits all too neatly with its self-image and which covers over any aspects they would not be happy with.

Accounting for oneself in relation to others

The exploration and analysis of the little life-world of a community that might be carried out by psychologists using radical ethnographic research will usually be focused on quite discrete and self-contained groups of people. However, there are many lessons to be learnt from wider-ranging anthropological and historical studies of cultures and subcultures, and studies that focus on the way the identity and otherness of culture is constructed and challenged are very relevant to our understanding of how relations of power – around such dimensions as class, gender and race – are maintained at a local level.

One line of work that is pertinent here is the historical study of the invention of tradition (Hobsbawm and Ranger 1983). Dominant cultures have an interest in presenting themselves as the natural rulers of others, and many of the ideological strategies of racism and colonialism have revolved around claims about the cultural superiority of a certain group. Italian Prime Minister Berlusconi's claim that democratic politics was a peculiarly European way of organizing society, for example, is bound up with a certain invention of the 'democratic' tradition in Europe as starting in ancient Greece and carrying through to the present day. Studies of the 'invention of tradition' have focused on the way that oppressed nations tell themselves stories about the past which are completely untrue factually (Scottish kilts that turn out to have been invented by eighteenth-century wool manufacturers, for example), but which have passed into everyday acceptance.

A second line of work is the examination of the dominant representations of 'other' cultures, and the way that these representations either portray the other as a barbarian incapable of understanding our tolerant democratic way of life or as some exotic specimen that is held in awe all the better to keep them at a distance. Edward Said's (1985) pioneering studies of 'orientalism', for example, show how certain cultures – particularly the Arab world – were constructed as 'other' to the West. This work is a kind of 'ethnography' of western culture which focuses on its construction of others. Even when they were idealized – as cultures that were sensuously mysterious – this had the effect of making them potentially dangerous to westerners precisely because they were so seductive. Another culture or subculture can be an object of fascination to an ethnographer to such an extent that all the researcher wants to do is to tell us how wonderful it is and how no outsider can fully understand it.

A third line of work is to be found in attempts to make sense of the struggle against colonialism and what it means for those involved. One of the outstanding figures in this was Frantz Fanon. Fanon, who was born in the French colony of Martinique and wrote about how racism wormed its way into the mentality of the oppressed so that hateful self-images became experienced by them as powerfully as by their oppressors (Fanon 1970). He worked as a psychiatrist and freedom-fighter in the Algerian war of independence, and argued that revolutionary violence is a 'cleansing force': 'It frees the native from his inferiority complex and from his despair and inaction; it makes him fearless and restores his self-respect' (Fanon 1967: 74). Fanon's ideas are not only still an inspiration for activists in the 'third world', but there are also radical implications in his work for how we think about the relation between those who do the observing and those who are observed by those in power (Hook 2004). Here the 'action research' dimension emerges as a violent contest between those who want to develop some kind of expert knowledge about their objects of study (very much in line with the history of colonial anthropology and ethnography) and those who fight back. Box 4.4 describes how elements of Fanon's anti-imperialist writing can be brought to bear on the question of ethnography (cf. Wilson-Tagoe 2003).

Box 4.4   *Theoretical resource link to anti-colonialism*

These are six elements of a critique of colonialism and internal colonization derived from Fanon (1967, 1970):

1   *Colonialism includes cultural imposition* – the colonial power makes its victims in its own image or in its own image of the victims. A subordinate community will then take on the value system of the community that dominates it. This means that 'cross-cultural psychology' that merely describes a colonized culture is very likely to be complicit in negative images of it. The internal shape of a community, then, should never be taken for granted.

2   *Alienation often leads to hatred of self* – some of the worst aspects of colonial domination are manifest in the hostile things a subordinate community says about itself. Treating a community as an organic whole can then mean that the stories that the leaders tell are taken for granted. This means that internal conflict is concealed, and its concealment perpetuated by the outsider. Signs of self-hatred, then, call for an analysis of what has been internalized from those with power.

3   *Recognition is a political issue* – lack of acknowledgement and respect by a dominant community will function to exclude and control. Withdrawal of recognition from another is a way of cutting them out from what counts as human. The flipside of this is that to give respect to 'leaders' willing to mediate between the community and researchers from the outside will always ratify or oppose local forms of power in a community, and may further obscure and subjugate components of the community in question.

4 *'Primitivizing' is one of the tactics that creates dependency* – pretending to speak in the style of a subordinate community all the more efficiently puts them in their place. The outsider who wants to become an insider may make their target community fulfil the expectations they have imported. It means that humouring a community can cover over conflict, including conflict with the outsider. When a community appears 'dependent', then, it is always in relation to the dominant community and what they want.

5 *Liberated consciousness is the opposite of individualism* – the most revolutionary forms of 'self-criticism' are those that are communal in so far as they break open the enclosed individual mentality through which the colonial rulers exercise their power. When consciousness of oppression emerges through communal public self-reflection, the image of the 'community' or 'nation' changes. Collecting accounts from individuals alone, then, betrays the possibility of consciousness.

6 *Violence can function as collective catharsis* – a call for non-violence can function to enforce a 'compromise' that means existing colonial power relations stay as they are. Opposition to conflict may be voiced by an outsider with the best will in the world, but this more self-satisfied option is designed to keep the things in the world and existing relations of domination in good order. Conflict resolution, then, may seem to solve a disagreement, but is itself part of the problem.

It is possible to carry out ethnography in such a way as to claim access to the real lived experience of those who are involved, but this claim is fraught with difficulties. We have avoided it in this chapter for two reasons. First, we cannot discover what individuals really mean through observation alone (Hamer 2003), and even ethnographic research that includes close observation and discussion with participants draws on their *accounts*, not their thoughts (Clifford and Marcus 1986). The second reason is ethical. Our ethnographic description is always to some extent fictionalized, with careful protection of the identities of those involved. We are interested in the structural features of a particular community and subcommunities, not the deep inner experience of the particular individuals involved (Augé 1995). Still less are we trying to explain what happens by discovering personal investments of individuals. Instead of idealizing 'individuals' or 'communities' we described ethnographic research here as something that can show us the contested power relations that constitute both of those things.

Further reading

Augé, M. (1995) *Non-Places: Introduction to an Anthropology of Supermodernity*. London: Verso.

Bhavnani, K.-K. and Phoenix, A. (eds) (1994) *Shifting Identities, Shifting Racisms: A Feminism & Psychology Reader*. London: Sage.

Clifford, J. and Marcus, G. (eds) (1986) *Writing Culture: The Poetics and Politics of Ethnography*. Berkeley, CA: University of California Press.

Willis, P. (1980) *Learning to Labour: How Working Class Kids Get Working Class Jobs* (original edition published 1977). Aldershot: Gower.

5 Interviewing

Interview research provides an opportunity to question the separation between individuals and contexts, to ground accounts of experience in social relations.

The paradigmatic form of interview for mainstream quantitative psychology is the 'structured interview'. The problem for psychologists trying to implement this paradigm as a technique of data collection is that it proves to be as impossible as any other approach in the discipline that aims for complete control over what 'subjects' say. There is really no such thing as a completely 'structured interview' because people always say things that spill beyond the structure, before the interview starts and when the recorder has been turned off. And all we have succeeded in doing if we manage to hold them fast to the question schedule is to force them to speak their answers to what is really little more than a questionnaire (Roiser 1974). We need to start at the other end of the spectrum – chaos – to arrive at a structure that might be useful. We will connect the perspectives we describe in this chapter later on with accounts of dialogical and carnivalesque collective activity that looks chaotic to an outsider (Bakhtin 1981, 1984).

The worst nightmare for quantitative psychology is an 'unstructured interview'. But much as researchers in this tradition might sweat about someone else taking control and creating something unpredictable out of an interaction with the researcher, this other apparently chaotic end of the spectrum is also actually more of a mirage than something that can ever really take place (Spradley 1979). An interview in qualitative research is always 'semi-structured' because it invariably carries the traces of patterns of power that hold things in place and it reveals an interviewee's, a co-researcher's, creative abilities to refuse and resist what a researcher wants to happen. The task of radical research, then, is to make the interview *an encounter that reveals patterns of power and creative refusal of a set research agenda*.

To make it like this we would need to do two things. First, we can turn interviewing from being merely a technique of data collection into a methodology, and craft that methodology so that it deliberately does some analysis in the very process of collecting the material. Second, we can focus on the interview process itself, so that what the interviewer says is treated with as much care as what the interviewee says. There are really two 'co-researchers' in an interview, and an attention to the intersection of two different agendas can help us question the way interview research usually 'focuses on the individual and neglects a person's embeddedness in social interactions' (Kvale 1996: 292). In this way we open up an individual account into something spoken in context and spoken against it. The process of opening up the contradictions between the agendas of 'researchers' and their 'co-researchers' also allows a dimension of action research to appear in the work.

Five key ideas in interview practice

There is no good 'model' for interviewing, but we can draw together some good ideas from different models. These four models, outlined by Burman (1994b), bring into the mix quite different perspectives ('ethnographic', 'new paradigm', 'feminist' and 'postmodernist'). They then – when a fifth dimension of 'resistance' is added – make it possible for the interview to be a place for different competing perspectives to emerge.

- First, an ethnographic approach to interviewing cues us in to the importance of an *internal frame of reference*. The interview always takes place in the context of some prior engagement with the life-world of those to be interviewed, and an ethnographic sensitivity to the scene of the research will enable us to make this into an explicit part of the interview process. Spending some time working closely alongside people before the interview and carefully noting aspects of their lives that will then appear as the background to the interview, perhaps explicitly as a topic of the interview, is crucial to ethnographic interviewing (e.g. Spradley 1979). We should also add the point that even when a researcher seems to come to an interview without having done this kind of work, the way the interview is set up still works as a frame that will appear in some way in the content of the material whether they like it or not.
- Second, a new paradigm approach will draw the interviewee in as a 'co-researcher' involved in setting out the background to the questions to be asked and making explicit the way these questions might be tackled, addressed or refused. The topic and the task of the interview is then negotiated beforehand, and there is *close*

attention to the way the agenda changes, either because the researcher has certain expectations – such as having to write a report after the interview for a certain kind of audience – or because the person being interviewed wants to get something out of participating. New paradigm research encourages people to participate in such a way that they too are empowered to become researchers themselves (e.g. Reason and Rowan 1981). In order to do that, the researcher needs to make the interview into a methodology that is open to the switching of perspective and positions between researcher and researched.

- The third approach, from feminist research, has a particular concern with gender, but gender appears in many different ways. Every interaction in western culture (at least) is suffused with assumptions about gender-appropriate and gender-inappropriate ways of behaving. Much has been learnt about the particular dynamics of questioning, negotiation and response when men interview women, and about the different ways collaborative research relationships are formed when women interview other women (e.g. Finch 1984). Feminist approaches attend to *how power is reproduced moment-by-moment as part of the interview process*, and the phenomenon of men interviewing other men is still also clearly marked by cultural assumptions about how it is appropriate and inappropriate to behave in line with dominant gender norms. The issues of sameness and difference between researcher and researched then have implications for other dimensions of power.

- A fourth approach has emerged from the discussions of 'postmodernism' in social research – the idea that our everyday life in this particular current phase of 'late capitalism' in the West is made up of a *multiplicity of competing stories* rather than one big story about progress and self-understanding that will fit for all (Parker 1989). Postmodernist approaches have been concerned with the variety of different agendas that researchers and those that they interview bring to a study, the anxiety that the researcher has that things will slip out of control, and the way each act of interpretation does violence to the lived experience of the other (e.g. Gubrium and Silverman 1989). When a feminist attention to power, a new paradigm focus on empowerment and an ethnographic exploration of the life-world of the interviewee are brought into the equation, we are led to reflect all the more intensely on what the political effects of the different stories might be.

- There is a fifth key issue, which is that the kinds of people we interview are not always those we want to empower as researchers. Interviews with fascists, for example, should not aim to turn over the research agenda to them so that they can say whatever they like (e.g. Billig 1978). In and against each of the first four models of interviewing, then, we need to include a perspective that challenges as well as charms. Here we bring in a political assessment of how dimensions of power between men and women, between oppressor and oppressed cultural minorities and between different classes, for example, call for an ethical position to be taken over what may be said. There are always *dimensions of 'resistance'* on the side of the interviewee, but a political assessment also entails some degree of resistance from time to time on the side of the interviewer.

One way of bringing these five approaches together into a radical interviewing methodology is to make the interview into something genuinely 'dialogical' (Bakhtin 1981), and to systematically explore the way we might 'interrupt' the way others are made into beings who are either the 'same' or 'other' from ourselves (Kitzinger and Wilkinson 1996). We will then be able to transform experience from something that appears to emanate from inside individuals into something collective that we all – researchers and researched – participate in and struggle over. The research then turns into deliberate, and potentially (but only potentially) transformative action.

Box 5.1   *Beware grounded theory*

The message that theoretical work is necessary for qualitative research has got through to many psychologists, but there is still a good deal of anxiety among researchers about the way that 'theory' seems to separate us from the things we find rather than bring us closer to them. This is where 'grounded theory' has come to the rescue, with the false promise to enable 'the discovery of theory from data' (Glaser and Strauss 1967: 1). Of course, every theory should be 'grounded', but the way it is set out in that approach is neither 'grounded' nor 'theory'. The problem is fourfold:

1   *Descriptive* – when the approach clarifies what is going on so that it seems that simpler things can be said about things that were complicated and messy. This hopeless striving for simplicity actually leads the researcher every time to say things that simply repeat covert assumptions from grounded theory itself.

2   *Saturation* – when it seems as if all that can be said about a phenomenon has been said. The researcher using this approach is then led to stop when the material has been 'saturated' by the coding process, and unfortunately other theoretical vantage points are then effectively closed off.

3 *Induction* – when the researcher comes to believe that the data 'speaks for itself', and that concepts and categories 'emerge' from the material. The claim that the theory is really only 'context-specific' – confined to the data – shows the hollowness of its attempt to throw light on what is going on. It adds nothing to our understanding because it has forbidden the researcher to step back and think about what they see.

4 *Objectivity* – when the knowledge is assumed to be 'out there' to be grasped if only the researcher can put aside all of their preconceptions. This leads to a version of 'objectivity' that requires that the subjectivity of the researcher is made absolutely blank (Parker 1994b). You can pretend to be blank and empty, but that pretence will just stop you from making use of what you know.

Glaser and Strauss (1967) wrote *The Discovery of Grounded Theory* for tactical reasons, to help sociologists doing qualitative work to formalize proposals for quantitatively-oriented research councils in the USA. However, the tactical intervention quickly slid into a full-blown strategy for research and then further down the slippery slope into old positivist-style 'procedures and techniques' that would reassure mainstream sociology that the 'discovery' of theory from the 'data' was not tainted by subjectivity (e.g. Strauss and Corbin 1990). Useful though the rhetoric of grounded theory is on occasion, qualitative psychologists should take care not to repeat its mistakes.

The next two sections show how the five key ideas we outlined can be worked together in a creative way to bring out aspects of individual and collective experience organized along the dimensions of sameness and otherness, and then how those aspects of experience can be challenged so that the contradictions between them become the focus of the research.

Questions with (rapport, narrative and containment)

It has been said that an interview is a conversation with a purpose (Bingham and Moore 1959). The way an interview really differs from most conversations, which do also have many purposes, is that the initial purposes are determined by the interviewer. What we have to be able to notice and reflect on, however, is how those initial purposes are challenged, cross-cut and sometimes subverted by the purposes of those who are being interviewed. The way the research questions are formulated at the outset will determine how the overall frame for the interview is set up and the degree of manoeuvre the co-researchers (the interviewer and interviewees) in this kind of study will have to produce something new.

A first research question should be concerned with the particular topic – *what do I want to focus on?* – and the reasons why this topic is of interest for practical or theoretical reasons. It is then wise, as a second research question, to consider the range of things that might happen in the course of the interview – *what might possibly emerge?* – and this is also an opportunity to think through issues of accountability and representation. Here you consider whether these interviewees will be from a group that you do want to give voice to, or whether there are reasons to be wary about what they may say about certain other groups, and you should consider what is involved in taking what these interviewees say and presenting it to your readers. A third research question may anticipate the way things you cannot directly predict might emerge – *what might be surprising about the interviews?* – the best research enables surprising things to happen (as opposed to bad and boring research where everything runs according to plan and all is exactly as we expected). The way these questions are framed will govern how far it is possible to develop rapport with interviewees, the freedom they will have to develop a narrative about their experiences and the security they feel in speaking about these things to you as researcher.

An example interview:

> This research focused on images of educational psychologists among schoolchildren ranging between 12 and 14 years old. Ethnographic and discursive studies have drawn attention to the way teachers in the area where the school was based have been concerned with the exclusion of certain pupils (e.g. Evans 2002), particularly young boys (Marks *et al.* 1995), and new paradigm studies have shown how relationships between pupils in class are highly structured (e.g. Morgan *et al.* 1979). Feminist research on power relationships between adult and child in interview research was important in thinking about how the interviews should be conducted and what might happen (e.g. Burman 1992a), and postmodern research in the field of education provided background on the role of language in classroom practice (e.g. Maclure 2003). The interviewer knew that schoolchildren are often likely to say what is expected of them to adults, but suspected that it might be possible to elicit some accounts of how adults, including educational psychologists, were seen within the school if anonymity could be guaranteed (Billington 2000). Those constraints and possibilities determined how the interview was conducted. The interview was conducted in class during a general studies slot in the timetable with three boys (who chose the names Arnie, Steve and Malc as pseudonyms) by an interviewer in his early twenties (Danny) who

had spent some time at the school during the previous two weeks as a trainee teacher (though he had not taught these co-researchers). The boys volunteered to take part after a class discussion in general studies about the role of non-teaching staff in the school, and this section of the interview is about 30 minutes into the 47-minute interview:

Danny: Ok, but what has this got to do with educational psychologists =

Steve: = the teachers [unclear] and with the psychos like when you're trying to explain ( ) Once they've made up their mind like [

Arnie:] like the teacher
exits you, and makes you go without even taking your coat =

Steve: = yesterday [in the general class discussion] I said this, and then the psycho is like so [mimics a female voice] special <u>special</u> and they're like the ones who'll send you to the special ( )

Danny: To the special school and the educational psychologists =

Steve: = my brother was sent, he sold his meds [Ritalin that was prescribed for the brother diagnosed with ADHD] and like [

Arnie:] you sold them.

Malc: He didn't. I saw Nob [a teacher] and he was talking to the psycho after.

Steve: Shut up.

Danny: Erm, how would you describe what an educational psychologist does to someone you don't know?

Arnie: He sold them (2).

Malc: He didn't. Me mam said they, like, live in Bowley [a wealthy part of the city] and she said they can take you out of school, and you go to a bin [
                            ] [unclear, laughter]

Danny: What? (3) What's funny?

Arnie: Steve let one off [farted]

Malc: You don't get it anyway, like where do you live?

Steve: And you, have you got kids?

Danny: What does this have to do with educational psychologists?

Steve: Why do you say that, they're psychos and like we're the ones who're stupid and they say [mimics a female voice] special.

Arnie: SPECIAL!

This looks like it is not perhaps the most successful interview if we are looking for some fluent structured argument, but it does highlight issues about the perception of links between use of language and class position. Notice that the banter is stereotypically masculine, and although this enables the researcher to seem to be best mates with his interviewees (Morgan 1981), things start to take a more uncomfortable turn (for Danny) at exactly the point when the three boys opt for some different kind of intervention than speech (when Steve farts and Arnie is still good enough to explain to Danny what is going on).

Two key 'steps' in the research were traced and retraced time after time by Danny. The interviewer takes care to try and find a way of asking open questions (*Step 1*). Some open questions, like 'what is an educational psychologist?' may simply invite the interviewees to give factual information. This information is not uninteresting, for it does show the kind of knowledge that is circulating and what they will convey in a certain way to the interviewer. However, the interviewer wants to generate the widest possible range of responses, and the formula 'tell me about educational psychologists?' was one gambit in this case. Because the interview is 'semi-structured' there is the difficult task of keeping the talk going without guiding it too firmly with leading questions, and so it is worth having a series of 'prompt questions' ready (*Step 2*). Prompt questions will include interventions like 'That is interesting, tell me more', 'Can you say more about that?', 'How would you describe that to someone who knew nothing about it?', 'What other ways would it be possible to think about that?', 'Can you go through that again giving some examples / different examples?'

We can see from this account that before the interview was carried out there was already an idea about where the questions might lead, and it was necessary to have some understanding of what the range of responses in the interviews might be. The trajectory of the interview could not be completely determined in advance, but the interviewer did guide the course of the conversation. Box 5.2 summarizes the most important stages of the process of setting up, conducting and getting ready to interpret an interview (see p.64).

Questions against (ideology, power and resistance)

There are some strategies for making an interview more interesting and for enabling the co-researchers to be able to produce something that is not limited by the 'purposes' that have been initially determined by the researcher. These six strategies work well in groups – the collective domain where more radical things tend to happen – but it is possible to adapt the ideas to individual interviews. This is where we turn the tables and make the interview into a space for other purposes than that of the interviewer to play their way out. These strategies are not mutually exclusive, and gentler or more direct versions of them may be appropriate to different kinds of interview situation and, beyond the interview, in other kinds of research encounter.

First strategy – invite co-researchers to interview you. The point of this strategy is twofold. It forces the interviewer to make visible their own assumptions about the topic, and it encourages the interviewee to elaborate other vantage points they might take as they try and think of questions to ask that might be relevant:

Steve:	So, Danny boy, your bonus for fifteen is what the educational psychologist does for her money.
Danny:	Well, I suppose it might be, like, a bloke, not only a woman.
Arnie:	I haven't seen a psychoman =
Steve:	= answer the question. What does she do?

Here we have things set up like a quiz with right and wrong answers, and there are clearly assumptions about the gender of the educational psychologist. At the very least, the interviewer's interventions now become explicitly part of the research and subject to analysis as intensely as the turns of the interviewee.

Second strategy – invite co-researchers to interview each other. This also helps the interviewee to think about issues that might be important as they frame their questions, and if the participants who are usually interrupted by others are chosen to be interviewers it may also enable a slightly more reciprocal relationship between 'interviewer' and 'interviewee':

Steve:	So, Malcy malc, when did you last see the psychy.
Malc:	When did Nob see her!
Steve:	Yeah, do the teachers have to see them?
Arnie:	They need to!

Here we start to see the functions of the different staff of the school in relation to each other being described. The first two strategies do not at all guarantee some kind of democratization of the interview, and the analysis needs to attend to dimensions of power that will always structure what is said and by whom (Burman 1992a).

Third strategy – ask co-researchers to focus on who this account is for. If our starting assumption is that an account varies according to situational demands and that an interview is a performance, then we need to make visible who that 'other' is that the interviewee imagines they are speaking to. This strategy aims to make explicit what the audience might be for the account that is being crafted in an interview:

> *Danny:* So, erm, who would you like to read this interview =
> *Malc:* = me mam.
> *Arnie:* Your mam is psycho [
> *Steve:*] she wouldn't read it. If I was on telly it could
> be like Crimewatch and like why do they make it worse, like the psychos like punish =
> *Arnie:* = cos they don't know what to do, like when Nob exits you.
> *Malc:* They wouldn't show it.

A grievance about unfair treatment is rehearsed here, and there is an indication of the way the separation between public and private spheres operates to conceal certain things that go on in school, and the sense that the boys have of the futility of trying to find someone to hear about this.

Fourth strategy – ask co-researchers to speak in role. This strategy also brings into focus the way that someone performs a role when they are in an interaction, but it does this through accessing the different kinds of account that the speaker is aware of by asking them to take up a different role so they can articulate that account:

> *Malc:* Steve you are very special and that is why I am a psychologist. I am here to help you. I =
> *Steve:* = Mr Danny, ok, I'm traffic, no, police [
> *Malc:*] to tell you how special you are.

Another representation of what perceptions of the motives of the educational psychologist circulate among the boys is made more evident here. But we cannot claim more than that this is but one of the representations. The third and fourth strategies do not aim for an 'authentic' account, and it is unlikely that an interview situation would ever be the place to enable something genuinely authentic to be expressed. Our theoretical assumption (derived from Bakhtin's work) here is that when we speak there is some kind of 'other' present for whom we give an account (e.g. Georgaca 2001, 2003). The most we can hope for is that we can make visible a greater variety of positions from which it is possible to speak about a topic.

Fifth strategy – provoke co-researchers. One way of encouraging interviewees to speak to us is to be very nice to them, but the problem with this approach is that we may just produce an interview that is banal and uncontroversial. This fifth strategy is designed to open up conflict and to bring to light contrasting perspectives on the topic of the study:

> *Danny:* So, if I can just be devil's advocate for a moment, you wouldn't need to see an educational psychologist if you behaved in class.
>
> *Arnie:* I'll be back [laughter]
>
> *Danny:* But you can't blame the teachers for calling in the educational psychologist if you don't behave.
>
> *Steve:* So that's it, the teachers need them, not us.
>
> *Arnie:* Nob needs them.

The teachers' use of the educational psychologist as a form of social control is actually made evident here by the interviewer as much as the interviewees (and this voicing of an assumption can be picked up later and discussed in the reflexive analysis).

Sixth strategy – focus on the deadlock of perspectives. This strategy aims to make differences of perspective between interviewer and interviewee explicit (and in group interviews between the different co-researchers), and to turn those differences into the explicit topic of the research. The deadlock of perspectives is the point where agreement cannot be reached, and then it is the task of the researcher to discover what that deadlock reveals about the nature of the topic of the study:

> *Arnie:* The way they speak in Bowley, like its crap and it's like =
>
> *Malc:* = they don't even understand us.
>
> *Steve:* That's why they give us meds
>
> *Danny:* Medication for ADHD [
>
> *Steve:*   ] <u>meds</u>.
>
> *Arnie:* You don't come from round here either.

Conflict for its own sake will not produce very much, though here it does make evident the perception of a link between geographical location, class and power (to prescribe medication at the very least). We do need to find a way of making the process of 'translation' in interviews explicit rather than covering it over and pretending that co-researchers are completely transparent and understandable to each other.

These six strategies are not designed to be prescriptive – as if this is what you must do to produce an interesting interview – but they do attempt to enable surprising new things to be said, and to remain faithful to the research questions while opening a space for people to challenge those (e.g. psychologists) who are usually positioned as experts on their lives. Interviews with children do pose particular problems for researchers (Moore *et al.* 1996), and the gender of the interviewer often turns out to be crucial to their success or failure (Willis 1980). This issue also intersects with the power a teacher may or may not enjoy in the classroom by virtue of her or his gender (Walkerdine 1990). However, the very difficulties serve to highlight processes that occur in all interviews to one degree or another (and an interview that seems to have gone badly, like the one presented here, can also be instructive because the messiness and conflicts are all the more evident). Box 5.2 summarizes the stages in the process of tracing a trajectory through an interview and making sense of what is going on so that we can provoke conflict and focus on contradictions along the way.

Box 5.2   *Stage by stage to an interview*

These six stages summarize what you need to do on your journey.

1   *Destination* – in which you choose where you think you might want to go and why it might be interesting.

2   *Map* – in which you study the layout and the way that others have represented the territory you want to explore.

3   *Route* – in which you compare the different ways people have tried to get there in the past.

4   *Guide* – in which you find some guides for your way through the new terrain and let them lead you through.

5   *Souvenirs* – in which you search for things that you can take back with you that will remind you where you have been.

6   *Recounting* – in which you recount your journey to others and advise them what they may want to visit and what they may want to avoid.

Remember that each stage will pose dilemmas, in which you will have to decide whether you are taking a luxury cruise that is designed to make you feel more comfortable, an adventure holiday that will give you a sense of heroic achievement when it is over, an exotic tour that will enable you to impress your friends as you tell them about strange practices that are not seen by many other people, or a pilgrimage to somewhere that you always felt some yearning for and which will bring you personal fulfilment. And each stage will also require you to ask yourself what those you visit will get out of it (something that is often difficult for most travellers out for a good holiday to think about).

Transcriptions (as thematic anticipations)

Researchers who conduct interviews often complain that the most tedious part of the work is the transcription, and this task is sometimes passed on to a secretary or friend because it is seen as fairly unimportant drudge work. It is possible to have the text inputted by someone else before going through it to check it against the recorded interview, but new researchers (at least) are encouraged to carry out the transcription themselves for two reasons. First, the process of listening again to the interview from a different position – away from the immediate demands to engage in moment-by-moment interaction with an interviewee – allows some distance, and you will notice things in the actual talk that may disappear in a transcription carried out by someone else. Laughter, friendly or mocking, sarcasm and reluctance, barely audible sounds – burping and farting perhaps – that may have significance are too easily glossed over by someone simply intent on getting the interview transcribed. Second, the choices that you make about transcription already require decisions that mould the text in a certain way, introducing interpretations that are then difficult to undo if someone else has already committed them to paper. As you make the transcription you are already translating from one kind of language into another, from something that was designed to be heard into something that is meant to be read.

What is it necessary to mark in a transcription? You need to indicate who is speaking, what emphasis there might be in the speech, points of interruption and overlap, moments of hesitation, a note about the bits of the interview you could not understand, and some explanation about other things going on that the reader might need to know to make sense of the text. This is the barest outline of how you might transcribe an interview to mark these things. It is easier to identify who is speaking by giving real names (the actual names or pseudonyms) before each turn. You can mark emphasis in the speech by underlining words or parts of words (and mark shouting with capital letters). Interruption can be marked by breaking that point of the turn that was interrupted with a square bracket and starting the speech of the person who interrupts with a square bracket directly below that line. Overlap between turns (where someone carries on directly, taking over a sentence) can be marked by inserting an equals sign at the end of the turn of the person who finished and the same sign at the beginning of talk by the person who takes it up and carries on. Hesitation should be marked with round brackets around a space, and where the hesitation is for a period over a few seconds you may put the number of seconds in those round brackets. Use square brackets around the word 'unclear' to mark the bits you could not transcribe, and square brackets again to indicate when there may have been other things going on (such as laughter, chairs falling over or mobile phones going off). Notice that in the example in this chapter some of the material in square brackets that seems only to explain what is happening also already introduces some interpretation.

The bits of transcript contained in the example interview sections earlier in this chapter illustrate how these elements of transcription notation are used. Notice that the turns of the interviewer should be transcribed with as much care as those of the interviewee. Each of these elements already introduces the perspective of the researcher and frames the speakers' comments in a particular way (especially when you are telling us what else might be going on that we cannot directly 'hear' as we read the text). More detailed transcription notation will be found in texts using 'conversation analysis', but you will then be producing something that is less accessible to a reader and will therefore also be introducing along the way a number of other theoretical assumptions about the way that language works (e.g. Atkinson and Heritage 1984).

The point has been made that transcription is already a kind of theory (e.g. Ochs 1979). The history of writing in western culture, which is interwoven with changing forms of thought (Illich and Sanders 1988), is a history of the steady accumulation of punctuation that aims to accurately represent speech (Parkes 1992). Early texts were written without any punctuation marks at all, and when we break up a text as we write it down we are organizing it in accordance with established conventions that do not necessarily directly reflect what was spoken. There is no such thing as transcription without theory, so the question is how you are going to make use of the theories of language available to you in a deliberate, reflexive way. Then, rather than unspoken assumptions about the way that you hear people speak creeping into your record of the interview, you can turn the process of transcription into an anticipation of the themes that you may want to highlight and extract for the analysis. Pretending that there is absolutely no element of interpretation in your record of the interview would certainly be an error that would count against a good assessment of an interview report (and Box 5.3 identifies other errors that you should be careful to avoid).

Box 5.3   *Marking out the pitfalls in interview research*

Things that should be avoided, and which would count against a good evaluation of a report, include the following dead-ends:

1   *You claim to have established 'rapport'* – no. Although you might yourself already have been persuaded by this claim before you tried to persuade the reader of your report, it overlooks the fact that the account given of what went on in the interview is necessarily one sided. What is of interest is not your mistaken idea that you have established rapport, but your attention to the moments when the relationship between you and your interviewee breaks down and what you make of it.

2   *Someone really told you their story* – no. How can you possibly know that someone you interviewed really let you hear their story? Stories are always crafted for an audience, and you should not get drawn into the performance so that you then relay it like some kind of gossip to your reader. What is of interest is not your idea that this is their real story, but what version of a story someone might have told you and why it took the form it did.

3   *You have discovered some important information* – no. An interview is not the place to discover information, unless you really wanted it to serve as some kind of interrogation in which you would match what someone said against what you already knew and then dig out more from your interviewee. What is of interest is not the 'information' but what the interview tells you about differences between forms of information and what the consequences of those differences may be.

4   *You use the interview to describe someone's 'experience'* – no. An interview may well be about experience, but it is an experience rendered into language, an account, and all you can work with is the account. To insist that what someone says in an interview is an account does not at all devalue what they say. What is of interest is what they have tried to convey to you by producing a particular account on a particular occasion.

Groupwork (as qualitatively different)

Most interviews in psychology are conducted one-on-one, and when we do things in this way we risk repeating the idea that psychology holds dear about human beings, the mistaken view that people do their thinking alone and only later tell others about it. There are some alternative traditions of work that we can connect with now, however, that make the motif of one-by-one research into something strange, as the exception rather than the rule. (These issues also help draw attention to some of the male-bonding banter between Danny and the boys, where Danny is drawn into validating what the boys tell him and the assumptions they are making.)

A first line of work comes directly from the 'consciousness-raising' activities of the feminist movement. Feminist perspectives in psychology challenge mainstream positivist research not only because the stereotypically masculine obsession with prediction and control is thrown into question, but also because the alternative engagement with subjectivity is collective rather than individually-based. Mainstream psychologists already know that collective activity produces a different kind of consciousness, which is why they are often so unhappy when women get together in groups. Qualitative research is now an arena where this knowledge about collective activity and the potential of groupwork can be put into practice (e.g. Wilkinson 1998).

A second strand of inquiry, which was influenced by the theoretical perspectives and practical experience of the women's movement in Germany, is that of 'memory-work' (e.g. Haug 1987). Memory-work is a group activity in which the participants work together – dissolving the distinction between researchers and researched – to explore the way elements of individual autobiography are grounded in collectively-structured histories. The littlest aspect of oneself is opened up in this work so the participants are able to trace how the way they experience and interpret it connects them with shared images of identity. Small details are treated as cultural artefacts, and the task is to locate these details in order to generate identities in social-historical context (Crawford *et al.* 1992). A collective reworking of the memory also changes participants' understandings of what a 'memory' is. (See Chapter 3 for discussion of memory-work in relation to reflexivity.)

A third line of research is to be found in the writings of Mikhail Bakhtin, whose work on dialogue (1981) and carnival (1984) in internal exile during the bleak years of Stalin's rule in the Soviet Union give some insight into what may have been most joyfully and progressively creative about the Russian Revolution. Bakhtin's work is connected with other key texts on language and Marxism during those revolutionary times, even with some confusion among Bakhtin scholars as to whether he was actually the real author of work attributed to others and whether he plagiarized much work published under his own name (Hirschkop and Shepherd 2001). This confusion is very much in keeping with Bakhtin's approach to authorship and language, and so it may be better not to tie the ideas down to one single individual and to refer instead to 'Bakhtin and Co.' It is now possible to read his work on the 'dialogical' nature of thinking – the character of individual human experience as always already embedded in a collective activity – in the light of his celebration of carnival as an open contradictory space (Good 2001; Mkhize 2004). The carnival, Bakhtin argues, turns everyday hierarchies and power relations upside down and inside out. Perhaps it is only in this carnivalesque questioning of the authority of experts who like to carry out research on others that a space for genuinely transformative action research can emerge. In the space of carnival the human being discovers once again its collective contradictory nature, and can take steps to change it.

Box 5.4 *Theoretical resource link to carnival*

These are six elements that make the interview dialogue more carnivalesque and open to resistance, derived from Bakhtin and Co.:

1 *Fiction* – the forms of reality that are produced in fictional writing and speaking are often more compelling than mere factual descriptions, and fictional accounts can reveal ideas that are dominant and those that are subversive. What interesting material might emerge if we asked our interviewees to leave the facts aside for a moment?

2 *Plagiarism* – the ideas that we circulate among ourselves are never entirely original; we borrow from notions that we guess will appeal to those we are talking to and frame them so that we will be understood. What reflexive possibilities might there be if we allowed our interviewees to try and make explicit the sources of their ideas?

3 *Multivoicedness* – utterances are composed of many different ideas at the same time, though the contradictions between the different possible sources and the different possible audiences are often covered over to make the utterance coherent. What might appear if we were to encourage our interviewees to bring these contradictions out into the open?

4 *Word struggle* – particular words can be the site of contest, meaning different things to different people, but the cultural, gender and class loading of words can be concealed if we take it for granted that we understand what someone means. What would happen if the interviewee was challenged over the meaning they seem to want to convey to us with particular words?

5 *Laughter* – one of the points of rupture in an interview is when there is laughter, of embarrassment or recognition, when something is revealed or something is covered over. What would we open up if we focused on the laughter and tried to interpret it at the moment it happened, and asked our interviewees to interpret it too?

6 *Embodiment* – another point of rupture in an interview is when the bodily presence of the co-researchers is made visible, not only in the physical location of each body in relation to the other but also in such things as burping and farting. What could we highlight as limits of the speaking if we treated these disruptive moments as playful and serious parts of the interaction between interviewee and researcher

It would be possible to avoid or limit these questions if we were to make sure that we interview people one by one, to prevent the interviewer from being outnumbered and to be faced with collective activity. (Why do you think psychology has usually opted for individual interviews in its research studies?)

The interview research described in this chapter has taken seriously Bakhtin's emphasis on the importance of fiction, and it has also borne in mind Kvale's (1996) scathing review of problems with interviewing, starting with the complaint that an interview usually focuses on the individual at the expense of social context. But even if we have succeeded in tackling that problem, there are plenty more in the minefield that we cannot be so sure to have skipped around so cleverly. Have we also avoided the following in Kvale's list: neglecting emotional aspects of knowing; making people sit and talk instead of acting in the world; making a fetish of verbal interaction; and producing boring collections of quotes rather than a compelling story that shows us something new (Kvale 1996: 292)? These reflexively ethical questions about the limits to action in our research always need to be on the agenda, and we always need to be on the lookout for something surprising in order to move from the same old story to something different: 'Just as the exception can prove the rule, so exceptional or incidental instances can function to highlight structural dynamics that underlie research encounters' (Burman 1994b: 67). Instead of aiming only to learn something about the person we have selected to be our 'interviewee', every piece of good research should also aim to learn something about the specific qualities of the interview itself, about why something was said and why something was refused.

Further reading

Bakhtin, M. (1981) *The Dialogical Imagination*. Austin, TX: University of Texas Press.

Burman, E. (1994b) Interviewing, in P. Banister, E. Burman, I. Parker, M. Taylor and C. Tindall (1994) *Qualitative Methods in Psychology: A Research Guide*. Buckingham: Open University Press.

Good, P. (2001) *Language for Those Who Have Nothing: Mikhail Bakhtin and the Landscape of Psychiatry*. New York: Kluwer Press.

Kvale, S. (1996) *InterViews: An Introduction to Qualitative Research Interviewing*. London: Sage.

6 Narrative

Narrative research explores how individual selves in capitalist society are performed, and it can show us ways out of the prison of identity.

From the 1960s there were many humanist objections to the way traditional laboratory-experimental studies in psychology dehumanized participants and also, as a consequence, presented a dehumanizing picture of the human being as a kind of clockwork mechanism. Traditional studies neglected the sense that people gave to their own lives, and humanist 'new paradigms' aimed to study that sense (e.g. Reason and Rowan 1981). The term 'narrative psychology' has emerged to capture the spirit of humanist alternatives to this demeaning image of human beings, and to find a way of representing the stories people tell about themselves (Crossley 2000). Here we focus on the way people *perform* their agency (Butler 1993).

In capitalist society people are treated as objects that must sell their physical and mental labour power to others. They are 'alienated' – separated from their own creative abilities – and a sense of purpose in their lives is then restricted to the little narratives they construct about themselves, and then to their 'identities' as secure fixed points of certainty in a world where the present seems to be dissolving ever more rapidly into an uncertain future. Instead of imagining that we are really finding these fixed points inside people's minds, narrative research can help us explore how the self is made out of cultural resources and how it feels as if our lives must have a certain shape with personal identity lying at the core (Squire 2000). In this perspective, *'narrative' is the performance of the self as a story of identity*.

The development of narrative psychology can therefore enable us to do two things at the same time, each equally important to capture the dialectical relationship between what we do in the world and the material we work with. First, narrative research respects each individual story and whatever shape of a life that emerges from a person's account of times of uncertainty and fixity. Second, we show how this sense of personal identity emerges as 'figure' against the 'ground' of culturally given images of the self, and how identity operates as a complement to and consolation for alienation. This chapter shows how we can study the way people perform themselves, and how biography may be remade in the course of an autobiographical path out of fixed identities as prisons of the self. When someone grasps that everyday performance of self as an opportunity to reflect on the limits of narrative, they open the path to carry out some radical action research upon their own lives.

Five key ideas in narrative analysis

These five ideas in narrative analysis hold the key to the way a story may be heard and retold by a researcher, but only if the dialectical relationship between these ideas – 'agency', 'temporality', 'event', 'context' and 'format' – is taken seriously. That relation between the five ideas holds them in tension in a particular manner at a particular point in history, so that individuals may tell their stories to others in a way that both represents themselves and reflects on the representations.

- First, one of our aims in the research process is to restore *agency* to the author of a narrative. Agency was stripped away from people when they were treated as if they were objects in mainstream quantitative psychology, and this 'objectification' of thinking and behaviour – breaking it down into meaningless measurable factors – produced a kind of knowledge for researchers that they thought was scientific, but nothing for the objects of their research (Billig 1994). The 'subjects' of narrative research, in contrast, are treated as exactly what the term 'subject' should denote. But there is an important precondition for being the subject of a narrative, which is that agency has a certain relationship to time, events out of their control, a social context and a characteristic way of relating what has happened so that it makes sense to others.
- Second, we open a space for a story to be told within a certain temporal frame, and we want to make that frame flexible enough for someone to talk to the researcher and for the narrative to be represented to a wider audience. The process of filtering a story so that it makes sense both to the author and to their readers may mean that it has a beginning, middle and end (Freeman 1993). However, we also make the *temporality* of the narrative a topic in its own right, so that alternative ways of reflecting on what happened may, for example, make an event in the past reappear as something new. Revolutions, for example, not only change the present but also change the way the past is understood, so that those who struggled against oppression are then included in a narrative that breaks

open the identities held in place by the old regime. But, this questioning of linear time is also designed to better restore agency to the storyteller so that they can give sense to what happened in context, in a certain stylistic shape.

- Third, narrative research is concerned with how someone relates events that are about something; that thing may be disturbing or incomprehensible, or it may be an event that brought about an unexpected change that was then viewed, or is now viewed, as positive. We term this thing *event*, and we mean by that something that intrudes or hinders, but which also then becomes a necessary reference point for the narrative. In this way narrative research makes salient the embodied material character of human life (Nightingale 1999). But, this positive or negative event is always seen as interpreted by the subject as agent, as woven into a certain causal structure, as understood in relation to other events and narrated within a particular kind of plot.

- Fourth, accounts given by individuals are always embedded in *context*, in certain kinds of social relationship and set against a certain kind of cultural background. A narrative is always already also a cultural narrative, and an individual or a group will rework available elements into a specific shape to produce something distinctive that captures and represents their own experience. Research into idiosyncratic stories needs to include some attention to the cultural resources that are used to make them distinct (Ahmed 2000). But, the context is, again, reworked in a certain way by the teller of the tale, in a certain order to make sense of specific events.

- Fifth, we study the way stories are told as narratives or worked into the form of narratives in the process of the research. The form of the narrative is as important as the content, perhaps sometimes even more so. The plot of a narrative is always organized around some kind of *format*, in a shape that may be immediately recognizable – as a scientific report or romance or tragedy, for example. The genre that is used to give a certain feel to the narrative also conveys something to the audience of how they should interpret it (Squire 1995). But, we also attend to the way the person who creates the narrative makes themselves into the author so that they can relate the events in a certain order, and how they use the story to make sense of things that happened to them.

People tell stories about particular things that happened to them or about the course of their lives in a certain culturally-specific way in capitalist societies, and this means that 'the comments of individuals should not be taken at face value, rather, they need to be located in wider structures of discourse and power so that their implications and ramifications can be fully understood' (Crossley 2000: 36). The order of telling, the puzzling about powerlessness in the face of external forces, the social relations that determine what counts as important for life and the style in which a story is told, are bound together so that it seems as if the individual storyteller is the centre, as observer and actor. Narrative research traces how these dialectically interrelated aspects of subjectivity are put together, and how they may be connected with the stories of others.

Box 6.1   *Beware interpretative phenomenological analysis*

One way of analysing interviews that has appeared recently in qualitative research in psychology, and which appears to offer a rigorous set format for interpreting what people say is interpretative phenomenological analysis (IPA). IPA presents itself as a 'method' that will be able to 'tap into a natural propensity for self-reflection on the part of participants' (Smith *et al.* 1997: 68), but its attempt to get an 'inside perspective' on the meanings that someone intends to convey during an interview – the 'phenomenological' part of IPA – leads to some particular problems when it is used alongside individualistic versions of narrative research (McAdams 1993). The problem is fourfold:

1   *The search for intentions* – in which the researcher believes that what someone says is what they really deeply intend to say, or they try to dig beneath contradictions to find the real intention underneath. This means that the actual structure of the narrative, the cultural resources being used, and the nature of the interview as a performance are wiped away.

2   *Naïve realism* – in which the researcher treats what is told to them or what they read in a written narrative, as empirical truth, which they then refer to as if it is real. This means that they fail to notice how an account is crafted for certain rhetorical purposes out of certain kinds of cultural resources, and for the researcher as a certain kind of audience.

3   *Constructivism* – which is an approach that is often mistakenly equated with 'constructionism'; constructivism in psychology is simply concerned with different perceptual and cognitive views of reality, and so it tries to discover underlying mental processes in the individual that construct things. Constructionism (closer to the way that 'constructivism' is used outside psychology) aims to show how the individual itself is also constructed.

4   *Reduction to the individual* – which is a way of viewing narrative that separates figure from ground so that we concentrate only on what

we imagine to be the 'inside' perspective. This means that we lose sight of how what is 'inside' is dependent on what is 'outside' the individual as the context for the narrative to make sense to us.

IPA is certainly an attempt to restore human agency to interviewees in psychological research, but it is too easily compatible with trends in narrative research that turn the approach back into mainstream psychology again. We would then be led to the mistaken view that the narrative 'is there all along, inside the mind', and that it is 'a psychological structure', so that the task of the interviewer is to discover 'the truth already in place in the mind of the teller' (McAdams 1993: 20). The search for intentions, naïve realism, constructivism and the reduction of narrative to the individual are all things to beware of in narrative analysis, or any kind of radical qualitative research.

The next two sections focus on the way we may research *'limited narratives'* surrounding particular events, and then how narrative analysis may be used for broader *'biographical accounts'*.

Shaping limited narratives

A first task of narrative research is to define the scope of the material. It may be fairly clear from the start of the research that the scope of the material will be less than a complete life story, and most narrative research does not have the resources – in terms of time and material support – to reconstruct a life narrative. Even the sketch of a life trajectory in narrative research needs to focus on certain episodes, and most narrative analysis is concerned with strictly delimited stretches of time. There are a number of research questions you need to clarify before undertaking any interview or analysis of already written material for a limited narrative. In this chapter we will be focusing on narratives derived from interviews. (For a fuller discussion of analysis of other kinds of text see Chapters 7 and 8.) First, *what is the narrative about?* It may be useful to formulate the answer to this question as a causal sequence as if it were the outline of a chapter, which starts 'In which ... [the person did this or that, or this or that happened to them, and what other sequences of events occurred]'. Second, *what is the author aiming to convey?* The storyteller may want to impart a message or moral to an audience, and it may be useful to sketch out what that may be in the form of 'And so we see that ... [they discovered this or that about themselves, or we have learnt this or that about the relationships]'. Third, *what are the limits?* You need to know what kind of limits you will need to respect so that the *telling* of the story can be brought to a close. Sketching a preliminary response to the first two research questions can help tackle this third question, but it may also be useful to anticipate adjacent areas that you will not be asking about.

An example summary of narrative:

> In which Jan took part in an experiment when she went for a degree course admission interview, and was told by the researcher that she was 'unusual', but there was something the experimenter did not know. And so we see that there is a difference between what psychologists know and what we know about ourselves.

Here we see displayed answers to the first two research questions, and we knew from preliminary discussion with Jan before the interview that the thing the experimenter did not know was not something terribly traumatic that she would find difficult to talk about (and so we surmised that there would be some limits to the telling of the story). This summary only briefly sketches how the episode unfolded in the course of the interview, and how it came to appear as a 'narrative' with a certain shape. We will outline the process of the interview, which also contains the substance of the analytic process, and along the way we will be able to see more of the narrative. We will trace the process through three main steps, keeping in mind the key ideas of narrative research – agency, temporality, event, context and format.

Step 1 is to define this narrative as an episode located within a certain kind of *research problem*. In this case we can take our cue from Billig's (1994) discussion of the way reports of psychology experiments 'depopulate' them, rendering the actual people and events invisible. Billig's answer to this problem was to 'repopulate' the experiment by writing a little fictional vignette to bring alive again what might actually have happened. Here, we have a slightly different take on the same research problem, with the character Jan speaking in the first person, and our research problem is the way mainstream research excludes the actual experiences of the people who take part in them. 'It was funny', Jan said, 'the guy was hovering around the interview room, and he asked me to take part in this dual listening task I think he called it'. She went on to tell how she had to repeat out loud sentences coming through one earphone while there was interference from the other. 'The thing was', she said, 'At home I used to practise repeating what I heard on the radio out loud over the last few years 'cos I thought I'd like to be a radio presenter'. She did so well on the task that the experimenter told her, as he thanked her for taking part, that she was 'unusual'. 'Was that why they offered me a place on the course?' she said towards the end of the narrative interview. What we notice so far is that Jan presented herself as compelled to do the experiment, with little agency, but ends up with the narrative of someone who outwitted the experimenter, as someone who became an active agent. The key event at the beginning of the story was the giving of the label 'unusual', and Jan was able to show how the label was actually very different (it was because she had practised the task) from what the psychologist thought (that her perceptual cognitive abilities were unusual).

Step 2 is to ask how the narrative strings together different events or aspects of the main event into a *causal chain*. There is a difference here between the way the causal chain might be thought of as a chronological sequence of events – in which, for example, Jan being told that she was unusual was determined by her practice at home repeating what was said on the radio – and how they are put together in the narrative. In the narrative causal chain, for example, she takes part in the experiment (one point in the chain) and there was something the experimenter did not know (a following point in the chain). And there is a difference between the sequence of events when Jan told us the story and the way the events function as narrative. So, in the interview, for example, she started off by saying that 'Maybe I only got a place on the course because they thought I had some weird cognitive abilities, 'cos there was this experiment when I went to my interview'. In the narrative causal chain, however, what Jan is aiming at – that there is a difference between what psychologists know and what we know about ourselves – emerges from the story of how there was something the experimenter did not know (one point in the chain) but they offered her a place on the course perhaps because they thought she was unusual (a following point in the chain). So here we are starting to see how Jan positions herself as author and agent in the narrative, in a certain narrative temporal sequence, around an event as it would be understood by the experimenter but understood differently by her in the context of psychologists thinking they are able to find things out about people.

Step 3 is to identify the way the narrative is put together so that it may be read as a certain *genre*. This is a question that can be explored in the course of an interview through a reflective question about what kind of book or film this episode might be. It would be difficult in this case, for example, to write the narrative in the genre of heterosexual romance, for the episode is not structured around the fascination Jan had for the vibrantly masculine experimenter and how she eventually went on to marry him. She hints at something comic about the event when she tells us that it was 'funny' the way the guy hovered around, and there are elements of mystery in the way the 'unusual' cognitive ability she was attributed with by the experimenter was eventually explained. We arrive now at how we might characterize the format of the narrative, and we could suggest that it contains elements of science fiction (hints of strange mental powers discovered by the scientist), of comedy (his bizarre mistake), and of detective fiction (save that the person who thought they were the detective turns out to be deeply mistaken about what he thought he had found).

This is the account of one individual, but by locating her narrative in a particular *research problem* (*Step 1*) we were able to show how the little bit of single subjectivity that emerged in this story was put together, and how the narrative may be connected with the stories of others. By attending to the way the narrative was constructed in a certain kind of *causal chain* (*Step 2*) we were able to show how the story functioned to produce a certain kind of message, what the author of the story was aiming at. The identification of *genre* (*Step 3*) may also be an opportunity to connect the way this narrative is put together with other kinds of 'detective' and 'science fiction' narrative in psychology (Squire 1990). The narrative here is an opening for Jan to develop an autobiographical account that challenges the part psychology plays in alienating people from what they know. Box 6.2 (see p.81) summarizes the broader stages of the analytic process, including for this kind of 'limited narrative'.

Biography and identity

All narrative hints at the production of 'identity' and how it is performed – including the way it is performed in a research interview – but in a biographical account which encompasses a much longer stretch of life, the question of identity is often explicitly foregrounded. The three research questions still need to be tackled before the empirical part of the study is undertaken – what is it about? what is the author aiming at? what are the limits? – but the stakes are much higher. The first two questions are more difficult to determine for sure at the outset. The third question – what are the limits? – should be explored in some detail in a preliminary interview. Here we will focus on a preliminary interview, for which there is, of course, no transcript; instead, there is a summary of key issues and some reflection on them that point to how the research interview might proceed. Transcripts of actual interviews should be attached in the appendix of a report. (There is a fuller discussion of interviewing in Chapter 5.)

An example summary anticipating a biographical account:

> Jan agreed to participate in a study of personal trajectories of people who become psychologists, and how they change when they have completed their training. We discussed reasons why she said she felt 'ambivalent' about taking a degree course, and why she continued to worry about the power she held over others as normal or abnormal. Some childhood experiences of psychiatry that she mentioned as important were explored. We also asked her how she thought different kinds of readers of the account might interpret it.

There is already in the frame of the research study a research problem, and here the biographical account will itself be embedded in a broader causal chain that has been determined by the researchers. The questions for the preliminary interview were about how Jan might find a way of speaking that produced something novel, and whether there were areas of the biography that we should be careful to avoid. We also included some reflection on whether it would actually be better not to proceed with the full interview process, which we envisaged taking place as six one-hour sessions organized as different 'chapters' of the book of her life, as one useful structuring frame for the interviews (McAdams 1993).

First point of focus: *a 'genre-in-the-telling'*. It is important to anticipate not only what the format of a biographical narrative eventually might be, but also the way it may be told. This has a bearing on the decision to proceed with the interviews for a biographical account. For example, if the overall format of the interview is in the genre of 'tragedy' – in this case, perhaps, as the fateful mistake to train as a psychologist and the series of woes it set off, culminating in utter desolation – then it would be necessary to think carefully about whether the researcher was able to offer the support the author would need as they experienced that narrative again in miniature in the course of the interviews. The focus on a limited narrative from Jan (of the experiment in which the psychologist told her she was unusual) gave some indication that the genre-in-the-telling might be more comedic, or maybe in the format of a detective story. Her account of how she wondered what psychologists really did and then discovered the truth – that 'they don't really know what people think after all' – might have produced a tragic narrative, but one in which the psychologists were the tragic figures, not Jan. This would mean that the genre-in-the-telling would not itself be tragic. When we said in the summary of the preliminary interview that some 'childhood experiences of psychiatry … were explored', this was with a view to determining what shape the experiences might have as limited episodes, and whether it would be possible to keep them contained. There is a possibility that the genre-in-the-telling could be 'therapeutic', and this would mean that there would be a particular kind of call to the researcher, and the risk of sliding into a 'therapeutic' narrative (Parker 1998). In this case, the event was told as a joke, not as something traumatic that would be painful for Jan to relate in the interview.

Second point of focus: *the review and production of a 'moral career'*. The notion of 'moral career' is useful for identifying what the beginning and end points of a prospective biography might be. In 'western' culture it is often assumed that a person's moral career starts with physical birth or development of conscious awareness and ceases with physical death. However, it is also possible to conceive of moral careers as having quite short durations in relation to specific social worlds. One's moral career through a student society at college, for example, might commence with the first meeting you attend, culminate in being elected as secretary, and end with degree graduation which is when you leave the college. There might then be a 'moral career' in relation to limited narratives about life in society. The notion is also applicable to broader biographical accounts. For example, Harré (1979) drew attention to the way a moral career in Japan might culminate in an eventual point of recognition of success or failure, way after the physical death of the individual concerned. We do not need to romanticize this other culture to take the point that the way the trajectory of a life might be bounded does vary. In Jan's case we were focusing on the moral career of becoming a psychologist, and so we were able to anticipate from the preliminary interview that the 'childhood experiences' she mentioned – the most important being one in which she was told she would be taken to a psychiatrist by her mother because she told lies, which led her to puzzle what a psychiatrist was and why it would make her tell the truth – would be the beginning of the moral career. We were also able to anticipate that a final 'chapter' of the narrative would be the possible future abandonment of the identity of psychologist (which was something she promised herself every now and then).

Third point of focus: *the mobilizing of 'identity scripts'*. One of the most useful notions in narrative research is that of 'identity scripts'. In this case, for example, one of Jan's identity scripts is that of 'psychologist'. The research will then attend to two aspects of this identity script that are held in tension for the author of the account. The first aspect is what is perceived to be the identity of a psychologist – what kind of person becomes a psychologist, what personality attributes would be expected of a psychologist, what image you imagine them to have of themselves and what other people think of them – this collection of things is treated as a culturally available 'identity script'. The second aspect is how the image is taken up and lived out, how it is performed in such a way as to put a distinctive personal stamp on the identity so that other people are perhaps a little surprised at how you function in that category of identity because you do not conform entirely to their expectations. This performance of identity, then, entails the repetition of elements of the identity script so that it takes on some substance in its own right, and the improvisation of it in such a way that allows a little ironic distance from it (cf. Holzman 1999). We assume that Jan will be able to elaborate identity scripts for 'psychologist' and for 'psychiatrist', 'experimenter', 'scientist', 'academic' and the range of other overlapping characters that will appear in her narrative.

In this way we are able to anticipate, with Jan as co-researcher, what the format of the narrative might be, something of the context for her biographical account, key events, the order in which they might appear in the narrative, and how she presents herself as an agent taking choices. We would then be able to reflect on how the various elements of her recounted experience are put together in narrative, and how they may be connected with the stories of others. What we have described here could, of course, also be turned around and used to elaborate an autobiographical account in which the researcher writes about themselves (Ellis and Bochner 2000). The production of narrative when someone develops a biographical account should also be an opportunity for them to stage for us their autobiography (even perhaps partially so in a limited narrative). And because individual lives are made possible by material conditions and social networks, the discussion of any particular narrative should connect with broader narratives (even to connect personal revelation with social revolution). Box 6.2 summarizes the broader stages of the analytic process, including for this kind of 'biographical account'.

Box 6.2   *Stage by stage to narrative*

These six stages summarize what you need to do:

1   *Production schedule* – where you identify the 'research problem' and set out what might be interesting about it, including some reflection on how the possible narratives circulate in culture. Write a plan for the work.

2   *Auditions* – where you find authors for the narratives, those who you will treat as 'agents' able to discuss with you the impact of certain 'events', whether for a limited narrative or biographical account. Find co-researchers, actual or virtual (in life or in already written accounts).

3   *Casting* – where you anticipate in a preliminary interview what the 'genre-in-the-telling' might be for a biographical account, and what the boundaries of a 'moral career' might be. Check that these co-researchers will be right for a biographical account or limited narrative.

4   *Improvized scripting* – where you give the stage to the author of the narrative to rehearse and produce in a distinct form for you the kinds of 'identity scripts' that are important to them. Make time in the preliminary interview for discussion of these issues.

5   *Performance* – where you see elaborated the narrative in a certain 'temporal order' in the 'context' of other kinds of similar narratives, in a way that becomes visible to the teller as author and listener as researcher. Conduct the interview or the analysis of the written account.

6   *Reviews* – where you may finally be able to determine what genre of narrative has been produced, and how a causal chain has appeared in the performance, with an assessment of what is old and what is new about it. Write it up, including reflexive analysis and discussion connecting with broader narratives.

Narrative truth in context

The story of research in a report is also, of course, a 'narrative', and there is a conventional format for psychological reports that usually makes them conform to a certain genre, that of the 'scientific communication' (in which a hypothesis is formulated and tested so that conclusions can be drawn). This genre is more secure in quantitative research in psychology because the author avoids use of the first person, but qualitative researchers (unfortunately) often try to mimic that genre. (There is a fuller discussion of report writing in Chapter 11.) The narrative of a piece of narrative research, then, will include the usual 'chapters' – introduction, method, analysis and discussion – but its self-reflexive character as narrative, which could appear as a final section of the analysis as 'reflexive analysis', raises some conceptual questions about how it relates to the 'truth'.

We have already raised the possibility that a biographical account in narrative research could be produced by the researcher, as an autobiographical account. We can go further than this, however, to include fictional accounts. Culture is saturated with narrative, and many 'identity scripts' and formats for 'moral careers' are formulated quite explicitly as fiction well before being lived out as the truth by individuals and collectives. There is good precedent for the device of using fiction to bring to life the different kinds of truth of what it is to be a person in narratives of psychotherapy (e.g. Orbach 1999).

Narrative research does not discover what the empirical truth is, but rather how someone makes sense of an event that they may have had some difficulty in describing so that it becomes true to them. Not all events are traumatic in the clinical sense of the term, but many can have a 'traumatic' quality, in so far as something happens that is unpredictable and inexplicable. As some commentators on narrative in therapy have pointed out, perhaps the appearance of something incomprehensible, and the attempt to make sense of it by integrating it into a narrative, is the closest qualitative research can get to 'the real' (Frosh 2002). In this chapter we term those points when narrative might touch the real as 'events'.

The third issue concerns how little individual narratives might also be big individual narratives, and how they might then connect with wider historical narratives. For example, the adoption of what comes to be a well-known name may be entirely contingent, and it may then function as part of a narrative of the political career of an individual so that it produces an identity for this character singled out by others as a key figure, only known to them by that adopted name (and as if they were entirely responsible for the historical events that they participated in). Political narratives may exactly display how a certain image is picked up and turned into an identity by followers of the individual, who is then treated as an 'example' (Parker 1996). The task of the analysis is then to show how the story of this single subject cannot be understood without connecting it with the stories of others.

Truth is stranger than fiction, but the alienation and separation of individuals one from the other under capitalism often renders narratives of exploitation and resistance into no more than fictional accounts. Research that attends to how individual identities reduce experience to the level of the individual can open a space for the exploration of collective narratives so that the truth about injustice can be articulated and the material conditions in which it is embedded can be changed, through new dramatic revolutionary 'events' yet to be performed. An individual separated from social relationships performs a kind of fiction, a narrative as partial truth, and it is when collective events happen that its nature as truth becomes visible (Burman 2003).

Box 6.3   *Marking out pitfalls in narrative research*

Things that should be avoided, and which would count against a good evaluation of a report, include the following little bits of narrative:

1   *'They really told me their story'* – as if you were able to go 'backstage' in someone's life and they revealed something of the way it was rather than the way they wanted you to hear it. You need to focus on the way it was told as a performance, and ask what the performance was about.

2   *'I think it was therapeutic for them telling me about this'* – as if you were able to slide from being a researcher into being a counsellor, and as if something traumatic that you were digging out for public view could then be covered over. You need to avoid intrusion into painful private material.

3   *'They were a good example of what it was to be like this'* – as if a person presents themselves within a certain kind of category, and this means that you should interpret them as being of that type. You need to focus on how 'identity scripts' are used, and what the limits of an identity might be.

4   *'This is what they meant by it'* – as if you could decode the story they told to discover what they really thought about it or, worse, what underlying psychological processes would explain it. Stick to the narrative as built up out of cultural elements and given an idiosyncratic twist.

Reproduction and transformation

The emphasis in this chapter on the 'performance' of identity has been with a view to opening up the possibilities for transformation rather than the simple reproduction of what we study. The task here has been to use narrative ideas to open the way for people to do a form of 'action research' for themselves rather than waiting for an expert to come in and do it for them. People develop narratives to account for events and for times of uncertainty and change. This means we also need to reflect on what we are doing in terms of how individual change can be connected with collective change, how the form of narrative reflects certain cultural assumptions and how 'identity scripts' can be rewritten.

Early on in narrative research a decision needs to be made about whether the 'author' of the narrative will be one individual who is questioned carefully about the course of events, or whether a number of people will be included in the study so that a composite picture can emerge, perhaps of a collective ones. Usually, narrative research decides to focus on individuals, but many of the most important narratives we live by are collective ones, of class or nation for example. This more difficult process then needs to rework some of the main assumptions of traditional narrative research, which are based on 'personal narratives' as individual stories (Holzman and Morss 2000).

A useful methodological device in narrative research is to organize an interview around the motif of a 'book', and to ask the co-researcher who is invited to be the author of the narrative to work through the different 'chapters' of the book of their life (McAdams 1993). Of course, this is but a metaphor, and the arrival of books in the world was a function of certain kinds of technology; wide readership for books was made possible by mass production. Certain kinds of book devoted to an individual life story are also quite late arriving in western culture, and the horizon of the 'novel' as a life story is bound up with the formation of 'imagined communities' that determine 'modern' forms of national identity and nationalism under what has been termed 'print capitalism' (Anderson 1991). Now, this historical location of the novel and the notion we have of life narrative as like a book raises interesting questions about how we might tackle new forms of identity, including so-called 'postmodern' identities (Holzman and Morss 2000). It would be possible, for example, to better tap into contemporary forms of narrative by organizing the research around the motif of palimpsests, film remakes or interactive CD-ROMs. Against the insistence of clinical psychologists with too tidy minds that non-linear narrative is indicative of thought disorder, we learn from this rich variety of cultural practices that narrative does not have to be linear to be narrative. Radical research in clinical psychology, in contrast, studies the way normalization is constructed – performed we could say – in narratives of 'mental health' (Harper 2004).

The perspective adopted in this chapter owes a lot to the writing of the feminist philosopher and cultural theorist Judith Butler. For Butler (1993), the category of 'identity', which is drummed into each human being in western culture as soon as they learn to speak, is a crucial element in the reproduction of the heterosexual matrix that has caused so much misery to lesbians and gay men, not to mention heterosexuals. It also underpins various forms of religious fundamentalism, including Christianity as its model form. Narratives of 'gender' and 'sex' are repeated to the child and then repeated by them so that they become sedimented as an identity category outside of which it seems the individual subject concerned will not be able to exist. The subversion of male and female categories has been a focus of 'queer theory' and 'queer politics' inspired in part by Butler's writing. To 'queer' identity categories goes beyond identification of oneself as 'gay' or 'lesbian', and it disturbs the lines of division between the categories so that supporters of lesbian and gay liberation in heterosexual relationships, for example, can also be 'queer'. What this work does is to 'muddle the lines between queer theory and feminism' (Butler 1993: 239). Not only does it open the way to new political alliances, but it also disturbs many of the assumptions that psychology is founded upon (Gordo-López and Cleminson 1999). Box 6.4 describes how elements of queer theory discussed by Butler can be brought to bear on identity.

Box 6.4 *Theoretical resource link to queering identity*

These are seven elements of the queer theory challenge to identity derived from Butler (1993):

1 *Differentiating relations* – treat the appearance and experience of being who we are as determined by what we are not. Even what it is to be a 'child', for example, is determined by the activity of those around it who are 'adult', including those who then write mainstream developmental psychology textbooks about those they are not.

2 *Power, construed as a subject* – take agency seriously precisely because it makes use of power relations, not because it is the source of power. It is possible to be a nice person when one becomes a psychologist, for example, but one still operates as a relay of powerful practices of normalization and pathologization that are not nice.

3 *Subjected to gender* – masculinity and femininity are identity scripts that demand a choice for one or the other and obedience to them. This helps to explain why the first thought that usually pops into the heads of an audience for another dull psychology seminar, for example, is to ask if there are any differences between men and women.

4   *Reiterative and citational practice* – key terms that define identity are cited and repeated so many times that they seem to refer to real things. One of the ways psychology pretends to be a science, for example, is to publish papers that cite strings of other studies, and so reiterate the same old categories until they are taken for granted.

5   *Identification with a normative phantasm* – images of what seem normal, average or stereotypical identities are secure prisons of the self. To speak as one of a category allows you to present yourself as 'normal', for example, and if you do it often enough you will get through psychological tests so well that you will be happy to apply the tests to others.

6   *Racializing interpellations* – identity categories are also cited and repeated to form race differences and calls for subjects to take them up. Interpellation, as a call to people within a category, turns 'race', as well as sex and class, from being a process into a thing, and then into a racist industry for studying psychological differences, for example.

7. *Queer performativity* – The deliberate acting out and parodying of identity scripts so that they are questioned and transgressed opens space for resistance. Try saying, 'speaking as a psychologist' when you go to a party, for example, so you start to see how ridiculous the performance of knowledge claims are by those who really speak 'as' psychologists rather than as people.

This kind of research has direct links with 'narrative therapy', and the most radical kinds of narrative therapy have also been an important resource for thinking about how personal narratives are constructed out of cultural resources (Monk *et al.* 1997; Parker 1999c). There are still some unresolved questions in narrative research about how bodily processes can be articulated into a narrative account, rather than simply turned into a narrative 'about' the body (Yardley 1997) or about the unconscious (Parker 2003b; Dunker forthcoming). There is a danger, for example, that the reduction to 'narrative' could obscure the way lives are constructed in material relations of exploitation and resistance, and the way these aspects of context should not just be turned into another story (Newman 1999). However, narrative research developed in the way described in this chapter may help to bring history alive again so that it is not merely the recounting of the chronological order of past events. Then the work turns into action research, for the way we grasp the past has a direct bearing on the way we can break from the present and make the future.

Further reading

Butler, J. (1993) *Bodies that Matter: On the Discursive Limits of 'Sex'*. London: Routledge.

Holzman, L. and Morss, J. (eds) (2000) *Postmodern Psychologies, Societal Practice and Political Life*. London: Routledge.

Monk, G., Winslade, J., Crocket, K. and Epston, D. (eds) (1997) *Narrative Therapy in Practice: The Archaeology of Hope*. San Francisco: Jossey-Bass.

Squire, C. (ed.) (2000) *Culture in Psychology*. London: Routledge.

7 Discourse

Discourse analysis provides an ideal opportunity for studying ideology in psychology, if we read it right.

The early 1970s saw arguments in social psychology for a 'new paradigm' that would 'for scientific purposes treat people as if they were human beings' (Harré and Secord 1972: 84). A crucial defining characteristic of being a human being is that we speak, and so new paradigm researchers called for a 'turn to language' in the discipline and for the gathering of accounts from people that would show a researcher the social rules and roles at work in little social worlds – of the classroom or the football terrace, for example (Marsh *et al.* 1974). This turn to language was the setting for the emergence during the 1980s in developmental and social psychology, and then in other parts of psychology, of studies of how the language we speak is organized in patterns of discourse (e.g. Henriques *et al.* 1984).

Patterns of discourse in capitalist society hold in place chains of demeaning images of human beings divided from each other on the basis of different categories (of class and race, for example). These images are repeated across the many kinds of text we encounter each day – in advertising, television news and mainstream psychology reports – so that we live them out and come to believe them to be true, of others and ourselves (Burman *et al.* 1996). These images also require certain kinds of relationship between people, the social bonds that confirm to participants that this is the way the world is (and that perhaps it is the way it should be). Discourse working in this kind of way is the stuff of ideology, and so *'discourse' is the organization of language into certain kinds of social bond.*

The 'turn to discourse' has immense implications for how we do psychology, for it encourages us to explore how we use and are used by language in society and it enables us to rethink how individuals are positioned in relations of power as 'subjects' by different kinds of language (Davies 2000). The analysis of discourse, then, can be very useful for showing how powerful images of the self and the world circulate in society (and in psychology), and for opening a way to question and resist those images (Willig 1999). This chapter shows how we can put discourse analysis to work in the study of ideology in written texts and interviews, and then how we can go beyond speech and writing to study other kinds of textual material.

Four key ideas in discourse analysis

There are four key ideas in discourse analysis that are useful for radical research. Some versions of 'discursive psychology' have now become part of mainstream psychology, and so it is more than ever necessary to link the concepts that we use in this strand of qualitative research in psychology with their historical roots in other disciplines. The importance of the first three ideas – 'multivoicedness', 'semiotics' and 'resistance' – is taken further now alongside the fourth idea, which is the study of discrete 'discourses' which specify versions of the world and the individual 'subjects' who are supposed to live in it (Parker 1992, 2002).

- First, we should look out for the *multivoicedness* of language instead of searching for underlying psychological processes or themes. This attention to the contradictoriness of our experience of speaking and being spoken of runs counter to most standard psychological research. In studies of 'attitudes', for example, the statements in a questionnaire that produce contradictory responses are usually dropped so that there is a clearer discrimination of the sole belief being targeted. For discourse researchers, however, this variability marks points of contradiction that need to be taken seriously. This is where the work of Mikhail Bakhtin (1981) is useful (e.g. Collins 2003). (Bakhtin's contribution is discussed in Chapter 5 in relation to interviewing research.) Instead of looking for how one particular word is the same as another, we look at how it is *different*. There is a difference, for example, between the description of someone as 'homosexual' or as 'lesbian', and both descriptions position the self and others as different in specific ways (Kitzinger 1987). We attend to how we are made to fit into certain categories and how are we marked out as different, and how the contradictions in and within the categories work.
- Second, discourse analysis focuses on *semiotics*, by which we mean the way we put language together in discussions and other kinds of text (in advertising images, journal articles or student essays), and how we are put together in a certain shape by the language as already organized into discourse. At the same time as we actively form sentences and turns in a conversation, we also have to use words and phrases that carry meanings we cannot entirely control.

This is where the work of Ferdinand de Saussure (1974) has been so useful, and where there is an opportunity to study visual images as well as the spoken or written word (e.g. Barthes 1973). The description of oneself or someone else as suffering from 'mental illness', for example, may not only construct an image of the self as a medical object but also construct a certain kind of career through the mental health system. Alternative terms like 'mental distress' might be used to try and avoid this construction (Parker *et al.* 1995).

- The third idea is that of *resistance*. Language does not only describe the world, it does *things*. Innocent comments may carry a force of blame or complaint or indirect request, for example, but these often deliberate uses of language as 'speech acts' are the very least of the problem for discourse analysts, for the speaker may actually be quite innocent of what discourse is doing. To look at power and resistance in discourse is a way of illuminating how language keeps certain power relations in place or challenges them. This idea picks up ideas directly from Marx (1845) and uses them to reveal how oppression is legitimized or challenged (e.g. Drury 2003). To speak of some small islands near Argentina as the 'Malvinas' or as the 'Falklands', for example, is to disturb or to keep intact taken for granted understandings of how the world is. Dominant forms of cultural identity are kept in place precisely by the banal ways the categories are repeated in everyday discourse (Billig 1995).

- The fourth idea that is useful for linking the study of multivoicedness, semiotic construction and resistance to power is that of 'discourse' as a chain of words and images. Here we treat 'discourse' as the organization of language into certain kinds of *social bond*, and each bond includes certain kinds of people and excludes others. There is something close to this idea in the description of 'interpretative repertoires' as patterns that capture how certain 'social practices' work. Some of the best early work on discourse in social psychology was developed as an analysis of racist interpretative repertoires (Potter and Wetherell 1987; Wetherell and Potter 1992). This then brings us closer to an examination of how discourse functions ideologically, how it presents an oppressive version of the world that may feel suffocating to speakers and listeners, and which shows no way out. For example, a discourse of heterosexuality defines what is deviant, a medical discourse defines what is sick and a dominant patriotic discourse defines what is alien. Within each discourse there are, of course, contradictions, and the way the discourse is constructed in specific texts will mean that it functions in favour of certain power relations, or perhaps against them (see Parker 2002, 2004a).

The preparation for qualitative research using discourse analysis needs to include historical analysis of how the forms of language in question have come to organize certain social bonds. This is important for two reasons. First, so that analysis of language in a piece of text does not treat it as if it came out of nowhere – for everything that has meaning for us has certain historical preconditions for it to be spoken, written or produced as an ideological image. Second, so that the text is put in the context of actual 'social bonds' or power relations – for everything that has meaning has a place in patterns of physical harm or well-being, of material oppression and the attempts to challenge it.

Box 7.1   *Beware conversation analysis*

One of the ways discourse analysis has been rendered more acceptable to mainstream psychologists has been to turn it into a version of 'conversation analysis' (CA). CA looks for patterns of social action that can be described in terms that are 'structural, organizational, logical, atopically contentless, consistent, and abstract' (Psathas 1995: 3). Once popular in sociology, this approach has now found its way into discourse analysis in psychology, where it reduces the analysis to moment-by-moment linguistic interaction (e.g. Potter 1996). It is possible to use CA to do interesting research (e.g. Potter and Edwards 2003; Potter and Hepburn 2003), but the costs are high. The problem is fourfold:

1   *Textual empiricism* – in which you only talk about what you can directly see in the transcript, with use of detailed transcription conventions that make it seem like you are really seeing what is there. This then means that if there is no direct reference to power or ideology in the transcript you imagine that you cannot talk about those things either.

2   *Pointless redescription* – in which you simply repeat what was said in the transcript in a more detailed way, and the use of bits of conversation analysis jargon makes it seem like you are being rigorous. This means that your points of critique are restricted to the points that are already made in the transcript.

3   *Nuts and bolts positivism* – in which you build up a stock of jargon terms, such as 'adjacency pair' or 'extreme case formulation', and make it seem like you are accumulating a more exhaustive knowledge about patterns of interaction. This technical ability to redescribe what people are saying then stands in the place of understanding.

4   *Not our department thinking* – in which you ward off any problems by repeating that your research question does not include the study

of ideology or power, because you are solely concerned with the orderliness of your little bit of text. This means that you seal off your domain of inquiry, just the way traditional academic institutions like it.

The interesting and useful work using CA carried out recently by feminist researchers (e.g. Kitzinger 2000) actually goes well beyond that approach, and necessarily so. It has to add a political standpoint and a critique of power relations in society, and it then arrives at an endpoint close to the radical discourse research described in this chapter. When discourse analysis is made into nothing more than a form of conversation analysis, however, it ends up looking uncannily like mainstream quantitative research in psychology.

The next two sections focus on how discourse analysis can be used to analyse ideology in already existing texts, and how it can be used as part of an interviewing process.

Discourse-analytic reading

There is no discourse analysis machine into which you can feed a piece of text; the analysis that is performed will be determined both by the kind of text and by the questions that are brought to bear on it. When we are dealing with a *'ready-made text'* – such as an advertisement, newspaper article or existing interview transcript – we need to think through the following questions. If these four questions cannot be answered, then perhaps this is not a text that you can analyse. Perhaps someone else can do it. These four questions anticipate important aspects of the analysis.

First, *why is the text interesting?* Something complex or contradictory must strike you about it. The text may set up a puzzle, and our first question then focuses on the way the contradictions work. Second, *what do we know of the material out of which it is constructed?* When we are able to say something about a text we draw on our own already constructed position in relation to it. In a text built out of shared cultural images, we have some kind of stake in it. Third, *what might be the effects of different readings of the text?* Everyday commonsensical readings and politically-attuned readings lead in different directions, and you will need to question the function of the text in its everyday taken-for-granted sense. Fourth, *how does the text conform to or challenge patterns of power?* The ideological force of the text may seem to point in one direction, but it may also attend to elements that point in another direction.

An example text:

> Mrs Thatcher goes to a restaurant with her cabinet. She tells the
> waiter that she will have chicken. The waiter says, 'What about the
> vegetables?' and she replies, 'They'll have chicken too.'

There is a puzzle about why it is funny, what political images it is constructed out of, what it is aiming at, and what the possible effects might be.
The advantage of a joke is that it is built out of contradictions within a little
world of characters that has been constructed very quickly, and it has an
overt function, to cause laughter, that may be problematic for some listeners. I have noticed that some women in the Discourse Unit that I have told
this joke to have not laughed. I wondered why. Because it is very little text,
it is also useful for briefly displaying some analytic 'steps' in discourse
analysis (Parker 1992, 2002). See Parker (1994c, 1999d) for fuller worked-up
examples and Wilbraham (2004) for an example embedded in theoretical
and political reflections on methodology.

Step 1 is to turn the text into words, relevant if we were dealing with
images or patterns that were not spoken or written; in this case we can
move directly on to *Step 2*, where we start to elaborate socially shared material connected to the text through a version of free association around some
of the questions we tackled when we chose the text. One thing we know
about these characters, for example, is that many members of Thatcher's
cabinet were men, and that she was often a figure of fun because she
asserted herself as a woman, 'hand-bagging' opponents, for example. *Step 3*
is to itemize and spell out the significance of the objects in the text –
'restaurant' (as a public place to eat food), 'cabinet' (as a piece of furniture
and as a collection of ruling ministers), 'chicken' (as a main meat item on
a menu), 'vegetables' (as an accompaniment to the main dish) – and *Step 4*
is to keep focused on how those objects are constructed in the text (cabinet
in relation to Mrs Thatcher, vegetables in relation to the chicken).

Step 5 is to itemize the 'subjects' in the text: 'Mrs Thatcher' (powerful
woman prime minister), 'ministers' (implied presence here as mainly male
members of the cabinet), 'waiter' (functionary of the restaurant), and, it
turns out, 'vegetables' (category of simple-minded person that Thatcher will
use to position her ministers). *Step 6* elaborates what else may be said by subjects in the text (along the lines of Mrs Thatcher's 'They'll have chicken too',
and corresponding statements we can imagine spoken by her ministers in
this text, as opposed to what we imagine them to say in the real world). *Step
7* spells out the networks of relationships for this little scene to make sense
– what characters are attributed with power, for example – and this can be
further fleshed out by *Step 8*, in which we can speculate how the characters
positioned in relation to one another here would deal with objections from
'outsiders' – if we as readers were to offer alternative viewpoints.

Step 9 is to draw out patterns across the text (in this case, that the ministers are transformed from being one kind of object, as members of Mrs Thatcher's cabinet, to another kind of object, as vegetables). *Step 10* contrasts the ways the same 'object' is positioned in contradictory ways of speaking (the 'vegetables', for example, are the kind of objects that are an accompaniment to chicken and they are also the kind of objects that we understand to be simple-minded persons). *Step 11* highlights how the ways of speaking may appeal to different audiences (waiters, government politicians and women). This then leads us to the bold *Step 12*, in which we name some 'discourses' as the kinds of social bond that make the contradictory arrangements between the subjects in this text possible – discourses of masculinity (whose standard these ministers fall below, to become less than men), of mental deficiency (into which category the ministers fall when they become less than men), and of woman's supremacy (as laughable reversal of what is often assumed to be the natural order of things). The analysis section of a report could trace the development of the reading through these steps (and the piece of text should be attached as an appendix).

Questions posed by a further six 'steps' to the analysis (in Parker 1994c, 2002) have already been anticipated in this account. These questions would foreground issues of power and ideology, and would link this little text to wider issues of images of men and women in political leadership (and how, for example, discourses of mental deficiency and femininity keep both of those categories firmly in place as fixed things to be mocked or feared). The text is designed to subvert a certain kind of power (Mrs Thatcher's) but in the process it confirms other kinds of power (including, psychologists should note, the easy use of a label to position someone as the stupid prey of the strong). Box 7.2 (see p.97) summarizes the broader stages of the analysis you would make of a text, including such a 'ready-made' text.

Discourse-analytic interviewing

In the case of an interview, the conceptual questions about a discourse-analytic reading will unfold and perhaps be answered by the person you are interviewing, your 'co-researcher'. Now it is they who are the discourse analyst. This still means that there needs to be some careful preparation and reflection about the topic, and in some ways this is a more difficult kind of research. Not only do you need to have done some historical work beforehand to clarify the conceptual questions – why you chose this topic, what stake you have in it, why you may want to question it, and what theoretical resources might be useful – but you also need to have determined that your co-researcher is also interested in questioning those issues and that they will be willing to engage in the additional task of helping you question their own discourse analysis. More than this, a discourse-analytic interview is a *'text-in-process'*, and so there are some complex issues that need to be addressed.

An example interview summary:

> Chris has agreed to be interviewed about images of 'addiction' that seem to him to be present in contemporary advertising, and which, he says, make a sensible debate about the de-criminalization of soft drugs more difficult. In part of the interview there is a shift to a different topic, which he did not expect, but Chris does still agree to discuss the analysis afterwards, and to have the interview included in the written report.

We will tackle four elements of technique here, drawing on 'narrative therapy' – an approach that is also variously known as discursive or 'post-modern' therapy – to trace through what happens in a portion of the interview. (See Chapter 6 for a fuller discussion of narrative research.) This approach treats a problem as a property of discourses that circulate around the client (Parker 1999c). We will, again, trace the analysis through the steps identified in the previous section.

First element of technique – the interviewee as co-researcher is enrolled as a discourse analyst. Chris already puzzled about the images of addiction, and so the first part of the interview is focused on what he means by the term 'addiction' (he said it is a 'label' used by politicians, and did not want to define it further). There were many hesitations here, and the interviewer shifted to a more useful question, which is how Chris had heard addiction talked about. He elaborated some answers (compulsion, finding pleasure in harmful things, weak personality types), and the interviewer asked for specific examples, taking each element in turn. At this point Chris mentioned an advertisement that annoyed him, for a fizzy drink that included a message traced out in the bottom of a greasy fast-food container: 'You need it because you are weak'. What the interviewer has succeeded in doing here so far is 'externalizing' the problem (White 1989). Note that this interviewing technique does not aim at therapy, but rather helps explore puzzlement about discourse. The questions that encourage this 'externalizing' are precisely questions about how someone can put their puzzlement into words (*Step 1*), wonder aloud about what the issue is (*Step 2*), and identify 'objects' in bits of discourse (*Steps 3* and *4*).

Second element of technique – the discourse itself is made to speak, and the analyst sees it at work. Steps 5, 6 and *7*, which ask how 'subjects' are constructed in a text, what they may say and what sets of relationships are assumed to exist there, are ways of homing in on what kind of person it is that may be 'addicted', and here a second element of technique from narrative therapy is useful (Roth and Epston 1996). Because we are taking part in a conversation with someone rather than sitting puzzling ourselves over some fixed text, we must help them make explicit what stereotypic characters are brought into being by the discourse. Fast food and weakness are among the objects specified in the advertisement Chris complained about, but the 'subjects' and what they would say is a more difficult issue. He said that the image was 'like a student flat, well like some sport student guys, maybe they're PE teacher-training students'. The interviewer asked Chris if he thought there were any women evident in the advertisement. 'No, well maybe they have girlfriends, they're not gay or anything I guess', Chris replied. The interviewer pushed into the second element of technique, and said, 'So, it's a world of young men, so what is it saying to itself, and to an audience'. (Notice here that there is also a degree of interpretation being offered by the interviewer, and she is 'constructing' something that Chris might then take up and make use of.) Chris took the cue, and in a mocking voice said, 'You can't cook, you're useless, and you don't care, you say so what, that's what they're saying'.

Third element of technique – a point of contradiction and space against the discourse is highlighted. Chris said, 'They're all off their heads young men, without women', and at this point he started to voice some of the ways in which a discourse disallows and discredits ways of speaking outside its own frame of reference, outside its own version of the world (*Step 8*). This brings to light a contrast within the discourse (*Step 9*) and different ways of talking about the same object (*Step 10*), which here is fast food as addictive substance. The interviewer took care to remain within a discursive frame. She was tempted to argue that in fact there were many women drug addicts, and many images of women junkies, but she was keen to encourage Chris to talk more about how he was positioned within these discourses as a young man. He complained about how the audience for the fizzy drink set up a space for men to want something but only on condition that they did so from a position of weakness. What they arrived at is a moment that might be seen in narrative therapy as a 'unique outcome' (White 1995). Chris started to describe the way health is marketed to men, as if, he said, 'you need it because you're gonna be strong'.

Fourth element of technique – the analysis is made visible to the co-researcher. The interviewer in this case summarized what she had made of this portion of the interview. A week after the interview she met up with Chris again, and discussed with a colleague the discourses about addiction she had identified in the interview transcript. Chris listened to the two of them, who were together discussing what Chris had said much in the manner of a 'reflecting team' that is accountable to a client in narrative therapy (Monk *et al.* 1997). The reflecting team is a device that makes the analysis visible, and here Chris was able to see how it might make sense to talk about discourses of addiction circulating in advertising. This made visible an account of how the discourses speak to particular kinds of audience (*Step 11*) and how we might name the discourses – as a combination of discourses of alienated youth, incapable men, and of compliance and protest both as indications of weakness – *Step 12*. Chris now argued that the fast food container in the fizzy drink advertisement might also belong to a woman, and that 'ladettes' were at least as important in drug imagery. This was written into the report, with the suggestion that these images of young women were constructed as if they were young men, and so were still functioning as images circulating in the same kinds of discourse.

An interview of this type should, of course, be with someone you can sympathetically explore issues with. (A quite different kind of interviewing relationship is described in Chapter 5.) It should be clear, however, that this does not at all preclude disagreement. The question is how the disagreement is handled and reported. Discourse-analytic interviewing which enrols someone as a researcher on their own language as a 'text-in-process' can be a useful element of participant action research, for it challenges the relationship between expert analyst and the dumb subject. Box 7.2 summarizes the broader stages of the analysis you would make of a text, including such an interview text-in-process.

Box 7.2   *Stage by stage to discourse*

These six stages summarize what you need to do.

1 *Spark* – for a ready-made text, this might be a text (or texts) that you find striking and puzzling and that you want to say something about, and a question (or questions) that you are provoked to ask by the text. The text could be something that presents a picture of the world and the kinds of people in it, and the question might be, 'What kind of person must I be for this text to make sense to me?' For a text-in-process, this might be a question about a psychological phenomenon that you will be able to explore with someone in and against it, that is someone already questioning how psychology helps make them who they are and how they might want to remake it. The question to be explored in an interview as a text-in-process might be, 'What kind of person must I be for this psychological phenomenon to make sense to me?'

2 *Ignition* – now you need to be very wary of taking things for granted, either in everyday assumptions that are made in a ready-made text or in appeals to your good common sense that your research participant in the text-in-process makes. Elaborate your suspicion that things are not the way they seem in the text, and note each and every point where you refuse to accept an assumption. An interview could be a place to encourage someone else to refuse easy assumptions and common sense.

3 *Combustion* – fragment the text into component parts by identifying the objects that are described (either explicitly or implicitly), the subjects that are referred to as active agents or as passive players, and the pictures of the world that we must buy into for this text to make sense to us. Ask what kind of people this text calls out to and positions as its readers, and what might be said by those who agree with things said in this text about those who disagree with it. An interview as a text-in-process can be the place to do this explicitly with someone else.

4 *Fuel* – now you are sitting with a text, and if you have done an interview, your text-in-process is now made (but not necessarily fixed). You need to know now what kind of theoretical stuff is going to get this motor running, and whether it is drawn, for example, from work on gender, sexuality, race or class as relevant axes of power. Maybe you have already opted for one methodological source earlier on, but whether you have already decided or are deciding now, you now need to put it to work. Soak what you have in this resource, and use it to organize what you now see in the text.

5 *Flight* – this stage involves a double movement. First, you accelerate and take some fast choices about the categories you are using so you can map what you see. These categories, which are driven by the theoretical resources, might be ideological images structuring the text or aspects of control and resistance. Use them now to read and frame the whole text, and your task now is to persuade someone else that these are categories that work here. Second, you trace back from what you see now to where you have come from. This is your trajectory, and the question now concerns how you came to arrive here (and what you may have missed by taking this route).

6 *Landing* – if you have been working with a ready-made text your work is over (bar the writing of it into a story of the right shape for a report), but if you have been working with a text-in-process you can take the flight path back to your research participant and see what they make of it (and discuss and decide what you will make of what they make of it).

Thematic analysis and discourse analysis

Discourse analysis is not the same as 'thematic analysis'. Thematic analysis often unfortunately amounts to little more than a grouping of quotes from the material, and the better 'analytic' examples of the approach organize the themes into a structure that illuminates the material (e.g. Castaneda 1970). A thematic analysis does have some advantages over a simple 'content analysis' of material – which is a simple counting of the use of certain terms and the contrasting of levels of appearance of the terms between different texts – but it does not go as far as discourse analysis in its linking of terms in a text, in the theoretical distance it takes from what it describes, and in its conception of what language does to us. We can look at the differences in terms of the different 'levels' of analysis in content analysis, thematic analysis and discourse analysis, but we will see that very different things happen at those different levels.

First, there is a crucial difference at the level of *sorting and linking*. Content analysis restricts itself to the words that are actually used in the text, and this means that the analyst has to know in advance what categories they are going to use to sort through the material. A content analysis, for example, might pick up use of the word 'vegetable' in a range of jokes but will not really be able to say anything meaningful about how the word is being used. Thematic analysis will also be sorting and categorizing, but will be more sensitive to what is 'meant' by the terms. Herein lies one of the crucial differences with discourse analysis, for a thematic analysis must assume that certain words and phrases really mean the same thing in a close enough way for them to be grouped together. The term 'vegetable' might be sorted into a category of depreciation of other people, for example, but will not be able to go much further than noting that there is a 'theme' present. A discourse analysis, on the other hand, is concerned with how words and phrases are linked at the level of discourse. A medical discourse, for example, articulates what it is to be a 'vegetable' with developmental failure or mental degeneracy and how the term functions differentially in relation to other terms that may appear to be similar.

Second, there is a difference at the level of *phenomenological immediacy and theoretical distance*. Content analysis does not, of course, concern itself with what is meant by the terms it counts and sorts and compares between different texts. There is no 'phenomenological' grasp – no attempt to trace the internal shape of experiential awareness – of what the terms might mean to the speakers. For example, the term 'addiction' might be employed ironically, but this irony would be lost in a content analysis. Thematic analysis is very much concerned with how people seem to understand the meanings of the words and phrases they use, but it is so much concerned with this that it cannot tackle what effects the terms have beyond what people immediately mean by them. That is, the 'phenomenological immediacy' of the meanings of the terms and how they might be understood so that they can be grouped together in the different 'themes' makes it difficult to get a 'theoretical distance' from those immediate understandings. Discourse analysis, for example, would show how the motif of 'weakness' may link images of addiction with images of men, even though those terms may not actually be grouped together explicitly by the speakers.

Third, there is a difference at the level of *what the effects of language are.* Content analysis does not even start to address how the terms it counts are actually used, and so it cannot help us to understand how people are affected by language. To speak of someone as an 'addict' would simply be treated as a descriptive term and its force as a pathological label would not be analysed. Thematic analysis may be able to pick this issue up, but only if it is a theme in the text; if for example, someone speaks about how unhappy they are when they are called an 'addict', or if the term 'addict' is also used alongside pejorative descriptions of people as needing something because they are weak. Discourse analysis, on the other hand, treats the meanings of terms as deriving from the way they are articulated into chains of meaning that are independent of the speakers – even if the speakers may also actually mean those things when they use them – so that 'addict' can be analysed as 'overdetermined' (functioning simultaneously in overlapping ways) within different discourses (for example, of medicine, adolescence, masculinity and moral decay).

So, not only do the different kinds of analysis lead to differences in the presentation of reports, but the analyses also take us in very different directions that are not compatible with one another. Recent innovative work has gone well beyond speaking and writing, to explore how the physical organization of space is structured so as to enable or inhibit action (Parker and the Bolton Discourse Network 1999). It is important, then, not to slide from discourse analysis into thematic analysis (still less into content analysis), for it can then be difficult to get out of it again.

Box 7.3   *Marking out pitfalls in discourse research*

Things that should be avoided in discourse analysis, and which would count against a good evaluation of a report include:

1   *Idle curiosity or voyeurism instead of a research question* – so you are not clear why this material has been chosen, what stake you have as a reader in analysing it, and what theoretical perspectives you might use to make sense of it.

2   *Sorting into themes instead of linking into discourses* – so you simply group the terms into categories, and do not show how they are linked, perhaps beyond the intentions of the speakers, to bring about certain effects.

3   *Discovering what people really think* – so you reduce the things that are said to what the speakers really mean, and, worse, into speculation about what psychological processes or personality characteristics might explain why they said what they said.

4   *Discovering the only reading of the text* – so that the overdetermination of meaning is ignored, and other possible interpretations that might be made by other readers using other theoretical frameworks are avoided.

Semiotic patterns in myth

One of the reasons it is not so strange to enrol someone as a discourse analyst in a piece of interview research is that discourse analysis is an activity that is already carried out by many people in the real world. As an academic activity, it would not be possible unless words and images were constantly being reworked and reinterpreted. There are three lines of work on language that are useful to ground the way discourse analysis has been described in this chapter. Each of them concerns the way signs circulate in society, and the way people make use of them to create certain kinds of image of what society is.

The first is the study of 'verbal hygiene' in which people reflect on language and try to keep it neat and tidy (Cameron 1995). Discourse analysis is a process of reading which discovers each time, in relation to each text, how it is possible to move from being a passive reader into an active reader. What Cameron's (1995) analysis of 'verbal hygiene' draws attention to is the way that ideology works nowadays to give a further twist to one of its oldest tricks. The simple argument that language is terribly important, and that if we learnt how to analyse it correctly and reshape it all would be well, is already old news for many people. Campaigns for plain English on forms, letters to the editor about grammatical mistakes, the correction of accents, scripts for assertiveness and attempts to formulate politically correct policies are testimony to the success of the message that discourse is important. The old ideological trick is to make people feel as if they are speaking independently just as they wish, and now, as a variant of this ideological trick, 'verbal hygiene is an interesting case of people acting as if they did in fact have total control' (Cameron 1995: 18). This means that discourse analysis needs to include the study of how people police language, and how they become active participants in ideology.

The second line of work concerns how people are called into a position by discourse and how an analysis of images can be useful in showing how that happens. Williamson's (1978) attempt to 'decode' advertisements has lessons for how we might decode all forms of ideological representation (in television, newspapers and films) that ask us to solve a puzzle in such a way that the answer includes the thought that this was meant for you. The positioning of people as members of a category so that they genuinely feel as if they are addressed and able to speak as an active 'subject' is also how ideology works. This is 'interpellation' – defined as a call to a reader of a certain type – and is most perfectly illustrated by the advertisements for lovely kitchens with a white cut-out space in the shape of a slender young woman. If you are such a woman, or would like to be one, or would like to have one in your house, how can you resist answering the puzzle of the advertisement with the reply 'Yes, that is meant for me': in this way 'we are constituted as active receivers by the ad.' (Williamson 1978: 41).

The third line of work concerns the broadening out of analysis to include cultural images that circulate between advertisements, films and newspapers, and which sell to us an idea of what it is to be a good, knowledgeable member of a society (Barthes 1973). When we use the term 'ideology' in connection with discourse analysis we do not at all mean by it that there are people who are led into false ways of seeing the world and thinking about it (as those suffering from 'false consciousness') and others who are able to perceive it accurately (as those who have access to the truth). If that were the case there would be no need for discourse analysis, for we could simply tell people what the truth is (maybe repeating it over and over again until they got it right). The problem lies in the organization of discourse which structures certain forms of social bond, and these are the forms of ideology that we speak and live out in ways that may cause misery to others and ourselves. Barthes' (1973) analysis of 'myth' shows how certain forms of 'speech', in images as well as in written form, drum home the message that 'this is the way the world is'. It provides one theoretical resource for taking discourse analysis further and is connected with rhetorical strategies. Box 7.4 describes the ideological forms that Barthes identified in the concluding essay to his studies of contemporary mythology.

Box 7.4   *Theoretical resource link to rhetorical forms of myth*

These are seven ideological forms of myth in discourse derived from Barthes (1973):

1   *The inoculation* – in which a little evil is acknowledged so that a bigger evil can be let off the hook. A fuss about the fiddling of statistical results and the invention of an imaginary research assistant by Cyril Burt, for example, will both detract attention from institutionalized fraud in research and serve to reassure us that in the rest of psychology this sort of thing could never happen.

2   *The privation of history* – in which the past is forgotten so that
     something implausible can make an appearance. We are repeatedly
     promised that the next 'decade of the brain' or the next discovery
     of the gene for schizophrenia, for example, will magically from
     scratch solve all of the arguments against biological reductionism
     because the failures of the old research no longer apply.

3   *Identification* – in which each troublesome thing is reduced to
     what we already know or put in a place for those that cannot be
     understood. The essential characteristics of men and women,
     and homosexual varieties of each, for example, are put in secure
     categories so we keep asking if there are any sex differences or treat
     those who seem happy without the identity of a gay or a lesbian as
     if they were curious anomalies.

4   *Tautology* – in which reasoned argument is abandoned in favour of
     the repetition of a statement as if it were now self-evidently true.
     We are told that a test for levels of intelligence must be targeting
     something because that hidden thing 'intelligence' is by definition
     what the intelligence test measures, for example, and so we are
     trapped in a fairly stupid language game.

5   *Neither-norism* – in which the attempt to choose between options
     is erased in the name of balance. A balanced view of fascism, for
     example, will conclude that it is right-wing authoritarianism that
     has many traits in common with or even perhaps different from
     left-wing versions of the same kind of thing, so the most
     psychologically sound position to adopt is to refuse either extreme,
     to refuse politics in research.

6   *The quantification of quality* – in which something is only taken
     seriously if it can be formulated in measurable patterns of
     equivalence and substitution. Someone's feeling about something
     might be respected, for example, but it will only find its way into
     mainstream psychology when it has been allotted to the domain of
     emotion or belief and factored into an explanation of behaviour.

7   *The statement of fact* – in which what has been challenged can be
     accounted for at a different level of explanation to keep it intact.
     Evolutionary psychologists are ready to agree that prejudice against
     other cultures is a bad thing, for example, in order to reinforce the
     message that underlying biological processes of competition
     between peoples will never be overcome.

Discourse analysis is not a panacea for psychology, and 32 problems are discussed by Parker and Burman (1993). The broader conceptual problems of a discursive framework for understanding the reality of exploitation are sometimes greater than the benefits of carrying out this kind of research (Parker 2002); it should *never* be treated as a substitute for political analysis (Jones 2004). An attention to reflexivity on the part of the discourse researcher is one way of tracing the process of the analysis (Burman 1992b), and of embedding a reading of a text in an institutional context in the spirit of radical research (Harper 2003). Not least are the ethical problems in much mainstream discourse research which does refuse to take back interpretations to those involved in the study. In the example provided in this chapter, this problem has been managed in a particular way to show you how this kind of research might work. There is an account of how the interviewee is involved as a researcher rather than being studied by the discourse-analytic 'expert'. This kind of analysis does open up points of connection with radical studies of ideology, and a way of connecting academic research with already existing action research, with the activity of people who are already challenging the way they are positioned by language and how they are subject to discourse.

Further reading

Barthes, R. (1973) *Mythologies*. London: Paladin.

Burman, E., Aitken, G., Alldred, P., Allwood, R., Billington, T., Goldberg, B., Gordo López, A., Heenan, C., Marks, D. and Warner, S. (1996) *Psychology Discourse Practice: From Regulation to Resistance*. London: Taylor & Francis.

Williamson, J. (1978) *Decoding Advertisements: Ideology and Meaning in Advertising*. London: Marion Boyars.

Willig, C. (ed.) (1999) *Applied Discourse Analysis: Social and Psychological Interventions*. Buckingham: Open University Press.

8 Psychoanalysis

Psychoanalytic research can be used to illustrate how what we feel to be so deep inside us is actually a symptom of life under capitalism.

Psychology has had a long-standing relationship with psychoanalysis, with figures like Luria and Piaget drawing on Freudian ideas to develop their own research. For many years that relationship has been carefully avoided by psychologists and we might even say that the psychoanalysis was 'repressed' (Burman 1994a). It is only recently that the emergence of qualitative research has put psychoanalytic ideas back on the agenda, with feminist accounts of subjectivity in heterosexual relationships (Hollway 1989) and of the development of masculinity (Frosh *et al.* 2001).

Psychoanalysis has also been popularized by Hollywood films, for example, as an attempt to address why we are unhappy by looking deep inside ourselves, when the problem is precisely that it was the separation of people from each other and from the products of their labour in the waves of industrialization during the eighteenth century that caused neuroses, experienced as forms of individual misery and unconscious protest (Parker 1997). Instead of taking psychoanalytic descriptions for granted, then, we have to analyse how they work and how psychoanalysis itself became part of the disease it claims to cure. This means that *'psychoanalytic research' is an analysis of contradictory pathological experience as itself already interpreted by psychoanalysis.*

What psychoanalytic research can do, then, is to turn psychoanalytic knowledge around against itself so that we understand better the way that psychoanalytic ideas have themselves encouraged us to look for things deep inside us as the causes of social problems. Psychoanalytic subjectivity – our sense of ourselves as having hidden childhood desires and destructive wishes – is the perfect complement to economic exploitation in capitalist society, for both succeed in making the victims blame themselves. This chapter shows how we can make these elements of individual subjectivity explicit, locate the elements in social relationships and so render them into things that can be broken open and transformed, in order to turn the research into a form of action.

Four key ideas in psychoanalytic research

Psychoanalysis makes a number of assumptions about the nature of human experience, of which we describe four here ('the unconscious', 'speech', 'Oedipus' and 'defences'). We must read these assumptions as arising from certain historical circumstances – the rise of capitalism and the privatization of relationships – rather than as underlying universal truths about psychology that were 'discovered' by Freud.

- First, psychoanalysis opens up *a domain of experience – the unconscious – that runs beneath and around what we are immediately aware of*, patterns and forces that we cannot control and which determine and shape our conscious thoughts. This conception of the unconscious appeared during the eighteenth century during a time when Europe was thrown into the maelstrom of industrial development that wrenched peasants away from the land and reconstituted them as proletarians who were indeed then subject to relationships with their new employers that were systematically mystified. In the unconscious we find patterns of relationships we are driven to repeat – in 'transference' to others. An attention to emotional reactions to relationships and unbidden 'investments' in certain ideas or outcomes of research – in 'countertransference' to those who may have transference to us – can be useful (Hunt 1989). At the very least we may fathom some limits of a 'neutral' stance toward our research topic.
- Second, psychoanalysis conceives of *a tool – speech – that may simultaneously identify and dissolve the work of the unconscious*, and it was only through the notion of the 'talking cure' that Freud was able to develop his ideas. Speech became a medium through which the analysand (the subject undertaking psychoanalysis) could connect things that had been separated and made unspeakable by the strictures that bourgeois morality capitalism demanded of its workforce and its managers. Speech is the place where what has been pushed away as a condition for being well-behaved can be unlocked, examined and made part of the real stuff of human psychology; that is, symbolic activity with other human beings (Forrester 1980). This notion calls for research and writing as publicly accountable activities. Even if psychoanalysis is treated with suspicion, it does add its voice to critiques of individualized expert knowledge.

- Third, psychoanalysis homes in on *the way human sensuality is moulded, compressed and replicated in a certain shape* through the Oedipus complex, so that we experience that sensuality as sexual desire locked up inside us and at certain zones of the body. The Oedipus complex (representing in its classical form a triadic relationship between someone who loves, the one they love and one who stands in the way of that love) is reproduced in such a way that certain kinds of sexual desire – that of the 'homosexual' for example – become prohibited. Eighteenth-century capitalism needed to keep this sexual desire restricted to nuclear families as engines for the production of new workers, but psychoanalysis noticed how all of human activity is suffused with desire. Some feminist researchers have read Freud as someone who gave a detailed description of how the nuclear family functioned as a modern factory for the production of masculinity and femininity (Mitchell 1974), and so how an attention to this offered some indications as to how those gender positions could be changed. Psychoanalysis as a prescription for how things *should be* is bad research, but it can be a useful ally for researchers who want to question how things have come to be the way they are and how we feel these things so intensely.
- Fourth, psychoanalysis specifies the different strategies – *defences – that are used to keep the truth at bay* and which lock together certain kinds of relationship and ways of talking about them efficiently enough to make everything seem under control. The 'defence mechanisms' used by individuals and by social systems will not necessarily be deliberate, but these little structures can be named at least, and employed by a researcher alongside other descriptions of psychoanalytic processes (Laplanche and Pontalis 1988). The reduction of human experience to the level of the individual and the illusion that people labour for others and consume what is produced out of their own free choice requires the operation of many overlapping defence mechanisms; strategies of defence at the level of the individual as complex as those needed by the nation states born at the same time as capitalist society. Description of defence mechanisms as conceived of by psychoanalysis is a first step to describing the social conditions that gave rise to them.

Freud was important to our understanding of how things come to feel so deep inside us because he was one of the first psychologists to notice how pathology is produced within certain kinds of social relationship. Psychoanalytic research can now explore how social relationships under capitalism brought into being new collections of symptoms. These symptoms, as little eruptions of unconscious protest at life in a dehumanizing social system, also draw attention to the fact that the ability of psychoanalysis to name those things is itself 'symptomatic' of capitalist society. We can treat psychoanalysis dialectically, as part of the problem and part of the solution; it is our way in and out of the contradictory shape of contemporary subjectivity and social relationships.

Box 8.1 *Beware the free-association narrative interview*

Psychoanalytic ideas have recently made a bid for power in qualitative research by way of the 'free-association narrative interview method', which posits a 'defended subject' as the object of research for 'understanding the effects of defences against anxiety on people's actions and stories about them' (Hollway and Jefferson 2000: 4). Here, 'meanings underlying interviewees' elicited narratives are best accessed via links based on spontaneous association', in which 'free associations follow an emotional rather than a cognitively derived logic' (Hollway and Jefferson 2000: 152). Unfortunately, in this case it is psychoanalysis rather than qualitative research that is in command, and the problem is fourfold:

1 *Individualizing* – when the focus of the research is an individual life story and the hidden underlying reasons why people do things. Common 'themes' are derived from different 'profiles', and the research ends up with society conceived of as the aggregate of individual psychological processes.

2 *Essentializing* – when the researcher thinks they really know what the 'emotional logic' of the free associations is pointing to. The 'cognitive logic' of associations in the interview is avoided, and the researcher then makes it seem as if they have actually found the emotional drivers under the surface.

3 *Pathologizing* – when the outcome of the research is a description of why people did reprehensible things as a result of certain unconscious processes. Certain past events or family constellations are used to build up a picture of someone in a 'psychosocial case study' that unearths the truth about them.

4 *Disempowering* – when the approach has the necessary consequence that for 'ethical reasons' the interviewees will not be told what the interpretations made by the researchers were. The researcher is the expert who only tells other experts what has been discovered.

A major problem with psychoanalysis as a discipline is that it is a master narrative that demands absolute obedience once it has been allowed in. Psychoanalysis is not content with being a culturally-specific historically-located tool, and those who use it all too often find themselves being used by it and made to evangelize on its behalf. It is a short step from using psychoanalytic ideas in interpreting what interviewees tell you to believing that you really do have 'knowledge of the way in which their inner worlds allow them to experience the outer world' (Hollway and Jefferson 2000: 4). Perhaps if you are tempted by this idea it is better not to use psychoanalysis to carry out and analyse research interviews, and not to let it get a grip either on you as a researcher or on your more vulnerable participants.

The next two sections show how psychoanalytic ideas can be used to identify mechanisms that hold together social relationships and the forms of subjectivity that inhabit them, and how those mechanisms can be redescribed in relation to broader societal processes.

Noticing and characterizing pathological differences

One way of tracking the analysis is to focus first on the way certain individuals or relationships are pathologized within a psychoanalytic frame of reference, how they are characterized as deviant from an assumed norm, and then to shift focus to the way this psychoanalytic frame sets up positions for the participants. This section will concentrate on the first aspect. The following section will shift attention to the psychoanalytic frame, and the way certain 'defence mechanisms' can be identified in the research material that are organized by psychoanalytic 'discursive complexes'. (There is a fuller discussion of discourse analysis as such in Chapter 7.)

Psychoanalytic research does call for some fairly wide-ranging reading of psychoanalytic texts, and the analysis starts to take shape through a to-and-fro between the research material (as the 'topic') and psychoanalytic material (as a 'resource'). As the analysis proceeds we move on to treat the psychoanalytic motifs in the research material also as a topic. A first research question, then, will be: *what do you recognize from psychoanalysis in the research material?* And, following on from this, a second question is: *what could be said about the way the psychoanalysis characterizes individuals and relationships?* The third research question takes its cue from the way psychoanalysis is concerned with 'pathology', and here we would ask: *what is marked out as different from the norm in this material?*

An example of research material:

In the film *Spartacus* (Kubrick 1960), there is an interesting subtext. The story of Spartacus has been an inspiration to many of those rebelling against capitalism, and the film itself has a radical image.

For example, the film credited the leftist screenwriter (Dalton Trumbo), and in doing so was the first major studio film to rehabilitate one of the victims of McCarthyism in Hollywood (http://pages.prodigy.com/kubrick/kubsp.htm). Let us turn to the subtext. Crassus (Lawrence Olivier), who is manoeuvring to become absolute dictator of Rome and so crush the Spartacus slave rebellion, chooses Antoninus (Tony Curtis), a 26-year-old Sicilian 'singer of songs', to be his 'body servant'. This episode is followed by some significant scenes, which include one in which Spartacus (Kirk Douglas) is reunited with Varinia (Jean Simmons) and rides off with her into the sunset, and another in which the present senate leader Gracchus (Charles Laughton) relates to Julius Caesar (John Gavin) this confidence, which contains a damning characterization of Crassus: 'You know, this republic of ours is something like a rich widow. Most Romans love her as their mother, but Crassus dreams of marrying the old girl, to put it politely'. A short while after is a 'bath scene', which was cut from the original film and the soundtrack for it lost. The restored version, released in 1991, has Antoninus' lines redone by Tony Curtis, and Crassus dubbed by Anthony Hopkins. The scene opens with Crassus in the bath. He calls to Antoninus. (The transcription here is mine, and you will notice that the text is a little cleaner than the everyday unscripted text presented in Chapter 5.)

Crassus:	Fetch a stool Antoninus. In here with it. That will do. Do you steal, Antoninus?
Antoninus:	No master.
Crassus:	Do you lie?
Antoninus:	Not if I can avoid it.
Crassus:	Have you ever dishonoured the gods?
Antoninus:	No master.
Crassus:	Have you refrained from these vices out of respect for moral virtues?
Antoninus:	Yes master.
	[Antoninus washes his master's back.]
Crassus:	Do you eat oysters?
Antoninus:	When I have them, master.
Crassus:	Do you eat snails?
Antoninus:	No master.
Crassus:	Do you consider the eating of oysters to be moral, and the eating of snails to be immoral?
Antoninus:	No master.
Crassus:	Of course not. ( ) It is all a matter of taste is it not?

Antoninus:	Yes master.
Crassus:	And taste is not the same as appetite, and therefore not a question of morals, is it?
Antoninus:	It could be argued so, master.
Crassus:	My robe, Antoninus. (2) My taste includes both snails and oysters. [Crassus gets out of the bath and walks into the main room, with Antoninus following him, and faces the window.] Antoninus look, across the river. There is something you must see. There, boy, is Rome. The might, the majesty, the terror of Rome. There is the power that bestrides the known world like a colossus. No man can withstand Rome. No nation can withstand her. ( ) How much less so a boy, hmm? There is only one way to deal with Rome, Antoninus. You must serve her. You must abase yourself before her. You must grovel at her feet. You must love her. ( ) Isn't that so Antoninus? ( ) Antoninus? (2) <u>Antoninus</u>? [He turns around to find that Antoninus has gone.]

The first task of psychoanalytic research is the *identification and representation of the research material (Step 1)*. The material here is quite long (about 500 words) and it includes some background to the film *Spartacus* and some portions of transcript. The material presented in a report should include sufficient detailed description, and perhaps (as here) bits of verbatim quoted text, so that the reader is able to make sense of it as it stands. Because this is an already scripted conversation for a dramatically staged piece it is cleaner for transcription purposes, and though this is rather artificial the lack of interruptions and overlaps do indicate something of the deference (on the part of Antoninus) and careful seduction (on the part of Crassus). Other more extensive background material could be included in an appendix.

Next (*Step 2*) we need to *note aspects of the character or relationship that seem strange*. We might note, first off, that the master-slave relationship does not permit a symmetrical open conversation between the two men, and Crassus' power over Antoninus already frames the scene as something strange, strange to us as viewers of the film. The questioning of Antoninus is rather peculiar, and Crassus himself is commenting upon some issues of pathology. It is not, he says, 'immoral' to eat snails, for it is a matter of 'taste' and not 'appetite'. Is the disappearance of Antoninus strange, or is it the behaviour of Crassus? In this case we see a series of metaphors being used to suggest something of a relationship with Antoninus that makes the homosexual desire of Crassus into something pathological.

Step 3 is to take forward that question of why a character or aspect of the relationship might seem odd by focusing on how *the difference between the characters renders one or both of them as pathological*. In this case, Crassus controls the course of the conversation, and shifts topic from stealing and lying to a taste for snails and oysters and then to abasement before Rome. Now, what is at issue here is *not* whether this might be a seduction scenario but how the seduction is being carried out in such a way as to position Crassus as pathological in some way. The psychoanalytic focus here is on what drives Crassus, and how he manifests his desire for Antoninus so that his desire is located in the frame of taste for snails and to be the figure of Rome before which Antoninus will abase himself.

We then move on to look at *how the abnormality might be characterized in psychoanalytic terms (Step 4)*. In this case, the dominant position that Crassus speaks from, and maintains in his 'identification' with Rome, means that he does not simply appear as 'feminine'. The picture is more complex than that, and it draws attention to something of the nature of Crassus as more perverse.

However, we need to take care to attend to how the relationship is *constructed and moralized about (Step 5)* – how it is portrayed through particular cultural conventions which assume a certain moral stance – rather than making the mistake of moralizing about it ourselves. We are not using psychoanalysis to pathologize, but are analysing how phenomena that are already interpreted by psychoanalysis are framed so that they appear as pathological. In this example we already have some clue as to how Crassus is set up to be pathologized from the comment of Gracchus to Julius Caesar, and it is already done in classic psychoanalytic terms. We are told that unlike the 'normal' love that Romans show toward the republic of Rome, a love that is as if Rome were their mother, Crassus 'dreams of marrying' her. And his dream is more than that, Gracchus implies, for to speak of 'marrying' Rome is to 'put it politely'. The Oedipal dream of the boy child to have the undivided love of his mother is invoked here, and a moral frame is already placed around Crassus through which we will be invited to interpret his reference to Rome when he tries to seduce Antoninus.

The five steps outlined here need not be followed in a linear fashion, and you may need to loop back to the earlier steps again. The identification and representation of the research material, for example, is a first step that may be modified as the analysis proceeds (in this example when other aspects of the film may need to be included). Box 8.2 (see p. 116) summarizes some broader stages of the research process by which we arrive at a description of psychoanalytic mechanisms and processes.

From defence mechanisms to discursive complexes

One useful way of identifying pathological character traits or relationships is to use descriptions of 'defence mechanisms' from psychoanalytic literature. There are accounts of these mechanisms in standard 'dictionaries' of psychoanalysis (e.g. Laplanche and Pontalis 1988). The dominant forms of psychoanalysis in the English-speaking world often unwittingly make explicit the connections between defences and ways of moralizing about character traits, developmental deficits or pathological lack of insight, and so descriptions of 'defence mechanisms' in this literature are especially rich as a theoretical resource. Here we can use some of the detailed definitions of defence mechanisms given by Vaillant (1971) to make explicit what seems to be wrong with Crassus. Here we outline two 'complex reframing strategies' to take the analysis forward.

The task here is to show *how the defence mechanisms are used to structure pathological processes* (*complex reframing strategy 1*). One way into this part of the analysis is to dwell for a moment on the 'mature' defence mechanisms Vaillant describes – 'altruism', 'humour', 'suppression', 'anticipation' and 'sublimation' – and to use these as test cases to see if it would be possible to make sense of Crassus. The 'mature' defence mechanisms are supposed to be common in 'healthy' individuals from the age of 12 (until age 90 Vaillant says). The other groupings of defence mechanisms ('neurotic', 'immature' and 'narcissistic') are clearly not regarded as desirable. Crassus does not seem particularly 'altruistic', for there is no direct goodwill or benefit being shown toward Antoninus. On the contrary, Antoninus is being told to 'abase' himself before Rome and, by implication, to Crassus. There is, perhaps, some humour in the line of questioning, but not as a direct expression of feeling. There is an agenda here for Crassus, and the wordplay then reveals itself to be actually a form of 'wit', which might indicate some 'displacement' from the real thing that Crassus is getting at. The use of witty metaphors to set little traps for Antoninus, particularly when he does not have the right to challenge Crassus, also draws attention to the pathological tinge to what might otherwise be seen as relatively innocent 'suppression' (postponing things that are too difficult to deal with immediately), 'anticipation' (careful realistic planning) or 'sublimation' (the channelling of instincts into cultural pursuits).

So let us turn now to the slightly more pathological defence mechanisms.

'Displacement' is one of the 'neurotic' defence mechanisms Vaillant describes (along with 'intellectualization', 'repression', 'reaction formation' and 'dissociation'). The neurotic defence mechanisms are pictured as starting at about 3 years of age (and lasting until about age 90). They are, Vaillant says, also common in 'healthy' individuals, but they may strike observers of the individual in question as a little odd. Perhaps there is some evidence of 'intellectualization' at work here. For that to be present we would have to have evidence that Crassus was using formal abstract terms to cover over his emotions (as academics often do). If we take Gracchus' comment seriously, that Crassus 'dreams of marrying' Rome, we might interpret the reference to 'the might, the majesty, the terror of Rome' as indicating some 'repression'; that is some forgetfulness of what his desire is to Rome and its symbolic replacement by an image of Rome to which one must 'abase' oneself, an image of Rome with which Crassus identifies himself. There is more than a simple symbolic representation in place of what is 'repressed', then. Perhaps there is something of the neurotic mechanism of 'reaction formation', in which one may deal with some threatening figure by modelling oneself on them. The triumphal aspect of the identification with Rome, in Crassus' admiring description of her power, might also indicate something of 'dissociation' (as a temporary out-of-character delirium).

There are some worse, 'immature' defences – 'projection' (including prejudice and suspicion of others), 'schizoid fantasy' (private make-believe scenarios), 'hypochondria' (afflictions modelled on others ambivalently invested), 'passive aggression' (failure or passivity designed to have a negative effect on others) or 'acting out' (immediate dramatic behaviour to gratify wishes) – that could be at work, and these are the kind of defences that individuals supposedly use between ages 3 and 16. If Crassus was portrayed as using these defences we might view him badly, but we might also agree that they could be ameliorated or cured by, for example, 'personal maturation, a more mature spouse, a more intuitive physician, or a fairer parole officer' (Vaillant 1971: 116). Notice how every specification of pathology in a psychoanalytic frame includes specifications for how the person might be brought into line with what psychoanalysis takes to be normal. Already, though, we have been led to expect that Crassus is a far worse case, and we need to move down a level, to the 'narcissistic' defences, to get something that fits the bill.

The 'narcissistic' defences are those that are used by individuals before the age of 5. One of these is 'delusional projection', in which the subject experiences their feelings inside another or another's feelings inside themselves. Perhaps the direct identification of Crassus with Rome is of this kind, and what he then demands is that Antoninus should be as obedient to him as he, Crassus, is to Rome. Another is 'distortion' where there is a reshaping of external reality, and perhaps identification to the point of fusion with another admired person. Crassus' identification with Rome might be understood in this way. (The third mechanism is 'psychotic denial', which does not seem so immediately relevant here.)

The defence mechanisms identified so far characterize certain of the characters and relationships in the research material as 'pathological' in some way. We are taking a risk here, for this kind of analysis could be carried out just as easily by someone who really believes that psychoanalysis is always true and that Freud gave us the keys for opening up the secrets of any and every personal and cultural phenomenon. For them, the psychoanalysis would be a theoretical 'resource'. We have to take care, therefore, to reframe the analysis in such a way as to turn the psychoanalytic shape of the material itself into a 'topic'. One way to do that is to treat the material as itself already interpreted by psychoanalysis, and to show how the psychoanalysis that is woven into the research material is organized around 'discursive complexes'. A discursive complex is a way of describing something (an object) and someone (a subject) in such a way that 'the object simultaneously looks like an item in a psychoanalytic vocabulary and the subject is defined as a psychoanalytic subject' (Parker 1997: 69).

That Crassus should be depicted as using 'narcissistic' defence mechanisms in his attempt to seduce Antoninus is significant here, and draws attention to a pernicious psychoanalytic framing of what kind of perverse being Crassus is. For he is actually perfectly representing what Freud (1914) described the 'homosexual' to be in his essay on narcissism. For Freud, the homosexual man takes the position of his mother and tries to find another to love in the same way as his mother loved him. The 'femininity' of the homosexual, then, is given a nasty twist by Freud, for it makes the homosexual into a figure who will demand some kind of childish love from another man. We may identify the 'discursive complex' of *narcissism*, then, as the guiding motif in this scene (*complex reframing strategy 2*), and the analysis then calls for a discussion of the cultural images of narcissism and homosexuality that are fused in the film *Spartacus*.

Here we must treat this representation of Crassus and the other characters in the 'here and now' of the scene as constructed according to certain kinds of cultural and political agendas. The film was made at a time when psychoanalytic ideas were becoming increasingly popular in the USA, and also a time when there was increasing anxiety about the breakdown of the bourgeois nuclear family. Popular psychoanalytic accounts of this family breakdown included fears that the absence of strong fathers would lead not only to delinquency but also to a rise in homosexuality. The rise of 'narcissistic' character types was one key motif in later critiques, ostensibly from the Left (e.g. Lasch 1978). One of the fascinating things about *Spartacus*, particularly bearing in mind that the screenwriter was one of the leftist victims of McCarthyism shortly after the Second World War, is the way that Crassus functions as a kind of fascist demagogue, hostile to democracy, and this pathology is bound up with his homosexuality. One of the political effects of the film, then, as viewed from the present-day, is that Spartacus himself is repositioned from being a kind of socialist revolutionary (as he was for many Left groups during the early twentieth century) to being a democrat fighting for good old US family values.

The analysis of material using psychoanalytic research that looks at how 'discursive complexes' shape how the characters are positioned, and how we are then invited to read the material as we too are positioned by it, is also necessarily an analysis of the political conditions in which psychoanalysis makes sense to us (Parker 1997). That is, it requires a close analysis of ideology in capitalist society. Box 8.2 summarizes some broader stages of the research process, taking the analysis of the psychoanalytic mechanisms and processes forward to locate them as guiding motifs in social relationships.

Box 8.2 *Stage by stage to psychoanalytic research*

These six stages summarize what you need to do.

1 *Appetite* – where you decide what kind of dish you would like to eat yourself (snails or oysters?) and how you might tempt someone else to enjoy it. The reasons why something is appetizing to you, and why it might not be to everyone's taste, also need to be considered. Identify your topic.

2 *Ingredients* – where you select the things that will work well together, and where you make sure that you don't get some bad pre-mixed packets of stuff that contain ideas that will be difficult to digest. Some off-the-shelf products look good but taste very synthetic, and they may be past their sell-by date. Select your material (*Step 1*).

3 *Recipes* – where you look at earlier instructions for preparing the same kind of dish, so that you have some kind of idea of what you want to end up with and make some decisions about the ingredients you want to add. Find something you can work to as a model and decide how to adapt it (*Steps 2 and 3*).

4 *Mixing* – where you carefully knead together the ingredients so that they blend together, taking care to mix just the right amounts and especially not to put too much psychoanalytic theory in. Don't over-egg the dish. Make sure the original ingredients are still distinct enough to be recognized at the end (*Step 4*).

5 *Rising* – where you step back and leave what you have prepared for a moment to give yourself time to reflect on what you have done and what your guests might make of it. In what way does it fit into usual items on a menu, and in what kind of establishment? What assumptions are built into this dish (*Step 5*)?

6 *Assembling* – where you divide the mixture into forms ready for baking. The shape of the thing is important, and it is often worth

thinking about dividing it into easily digestible portions rather than leaving it in one big lump in the dish. Organize your account into clear subheadings (*complex reframing strategies 1* and *2*).

7   *Tasting* – where you go back to the beginning of the whole report and slowly digest it, savouring the nicely-cooked aspects, and making sure that undercooked portions are dealt with. The proof of the pudding lies in the eating, but make sure the menu follows a sensible order.

Consciousness, conversation and repression

The role of subjectivity in psychoanalytic research is crucial. Subjectivity is viewed by psychoanalysis, as with much qualitative research, not as a problem but as a resource (and topic). To draw upon one's own subjectivity in the research process does not mean that one is not being 'objective', but that one actually comes closer to a truer account. In psychoanalytic terms, the 'investment' the researcher has in the material they are studying plays a major role in the interest that will eventually accrue from the research. In Anglo-US psychoanalytic jargon the analyst's own investments and responses are known as their 'countertransference' (Laplanche and Pontalis 1988). What follows here are three ways it has been discussed that are relevant to qualitative research in psychology.

   One approach that is explicitly located in the US tradition of psychoanalysis is Hunt's (1989) discussion of the use of countertransference in fieldwork. For Hunt, the research process is 'hermeneutic' – an interpretative activity that aims for deeper understanding of the research material – and what happens to the researcher in the course of the research will be as important as what happens to the analysand (their object of study): 'The psychoanalytic narrative thus constitutes an intersubjective construction mediated by the shifting conscious and unconscious mental representations, transferences, and countertransferences of both analyst and analysand' (Hunt 1989: 29). Here, of course, there is an assumption that such things as conscious and unconscious 'mental representations' are really at work. There would be a risk here, for example, of treating the 'defence mechanisms' we identified in the *Spartacus* material as real things that we had discovered.

   A second approach has been adopted by the 'post-Jungian' writer Andrew Samuels (1993), who enlarges the scope of 'transference' and 'countertransference' to include all the mutual influences and effects of interaction between someone who wants to understand and change the world and the things in the world that resist understanding or change. Samuels' argument here is quite compatible with the position taken in this chapter, especially when he argues that 'the subjectivity of the countertransference is not an autonomous, "authentic" subjectivity – quite the opposite when we recognise that the source of such a subjectivity (politics) lies outside the subject (the analyst)' (Samuels 1993: 36). There is an attempt to make the analysis into something 'therapeutic' (and here I am a little more cautious about the approach for I would treat 'therapy' too as a culturally-specific activity). In this light, the analysis of the *Spartacus* material would be driven by the question of how we can make sense of it, including how we are affected by it.

A third position is advanced by Michael Billig (1999), who comes at the problem from outside psychoanalysis altogether and whose analysis of 'repression' turns it from being something mysterious inside the head to a process that occurs in conversation: 'Conversation demands constraints and what is forbidden becomes an object of desire. Language creates these forbidden desires, but also provides the means for pushing them from conscious attention' (Billig 1999: 254). Billig does not explicitly discuss 'countertransference', but there are important implications for how we should see the position of the researcher. The way we craft our account of 'forbidden desires' in research material will be profoundly shaped not so much by our own hidden 'forbidden desires' as by the way the language of research and report-writing works according to certain conventions. This means that we need to reflect upon how what we write will be interpreted by those who read it, by the 'investments' we imagine them to have as well as our own investments. Perhaps it is no accident that the metaphor of 'investment' is important to the language of psychoanalysis. After all, psychoanalysis did emerge at the same time as capitalist society in the western world. (It is important, then, that our investment in psychoanalysis is itself not too great.)

Box 8.3 *Marking out pitfalls in psychoanalytic research*

Things that should be avoided and which would count against a good evaluation of a report include the following slips:

1 *Taking for granted what psychoanalytic theory says* – this happens when a description of a psychodynamic process seems so accurately to account for something you are describing that you end up talking about it as if the psychoanalytic account were true.

2 *Telling us what the unconscious motives are* – this happens when a psychoanalytic account is used to disregard what people say because you are sure you know what they really mean, and worse still that you can explain it because of things deep inside them that they are unaware of.

3 *Describing psychoanalytic pathologies as moral faults* – this happens when the moralizing that is often used as part of the labelling of people by psychoanalytic writers is adopted by you because you have started to get drawn into the description as if it really were true of the characters it pertains to.

4 *Discovering developmental deficits or childhood trauma* – this happens when psychoanalytic speculation is used to construct a version of what a person's life must have been like for the psychoanalytic account to be correct and, worse still, to construct an account of things that happened then to explain what they say now.

Social representations of psychoanalysis

This chapter has argued that we should take psychoanalysis seriously because it is a powerful social phenomenon that structures how we think about ourselves and because it opens up new vantage points on things that we usually take for granted. It has also been argued, just as strongly, that we should not, as a consequence, take psychoanalysis itself for granted. Psychoanalysis is not the truth about ourselves that we have only now discovered but something that has *become* true, and could once again in the future become untrue. There are a number of different vantage points on this process of studying this strange dialectical 'truth' status of psychoanalysis.

First, within the tradition of European social psychology an important study by Serge Moscovici (1976) of psychoanalysis in 1950s France illustrated how newspapers and other media were then starting to use psychoanalytic terminology to describe individual motives and political events. This path-breaking work also showed how popular descriptions of the 'ego', 'unconscious' and suchlike function as 'social representations', which operate, like all representations, *'to make something familiar, or unfamiliarity itself, familiar'* (Moscovici 1984: 24). Social representations of psychoanalysis have continued to increase since the 1950s, of course, and every weird formulation in psychoanalytic theory can be made into something familiar by simplifying it and repeating it in the popular press. Psychoanalytic research includes, of course, research into the spread of the social representations of psychoanalysis and the way that people use them.

Second, psychoanalysis permeates everyday life not only through the images of analysts and patients in Hollywood films but also in the increasing influence of psychotherapy as a profession. It could be argued that psychoanalysis has become prevalent as a 'representation' of the self while its actual material effect on people is very small. On the other hand, the truth may be exactly the reverse; that the explicit images of psychoanalysis are quite thinly spread in our culture compared with the power that psycho-analysis enjoys as a practice in therapy, social work and welfare services. The 'professionalization' of psychotherapy, then, needs to be taken very seriously because it is one way that particular versions of psychoanalysis are tightening their grip on the way we are categorized and treated (House 2002).

Third, and finally, there is a radical critique of mainstream English-speaking psychoanalysis from within the psychoanalytic movement developed by the French analyst Jacques Lacan. The focus on defence mechanisms that would enable the ego to adapt more or less well to society was, for Lacan, a betrayal of psychoanalysis. Psychoanalysis should concern itself with the impossible gap in human experience that is the unconscious, and he railed against 'those active practitioners of orthopaedics that the analysts of the second and third generations became, busying themselves, by psychologising analytic theory, in stitching up this gap' (Lacan 1979: 23). Lacan's critique draws attention to the way US psychoanalysis and psychoanalysis in the British tradition reflect common-sense assumptions about what psychology is and simply reflect dominant assumptions from the culture in which they work. Lacan's take on psychoanalysis, then, makes it the opposite of psychology (Parker 2003c), and there are also some important consequences for psychoanalytic research that includes reflection upon the role of the researcher. Box 8.4 describes how elements of Lacanian theory may be usefully employed.

Box 8.4   *Theoretical resource link to Lacanian psychoanalysis*

These are six elements for psychoanalytic research derived from the writings of Lacan (1979):

1   *Analysis is a process* – the task of the analyst is not to rummage around in the material and dig out the correct interpretation, but to act as a catalyst for the analysis to appear. Boxes and flow diagrams in cognitive psychology, for example, make it seem as if something has been fixed in human thinking, but all that has been fixed is the impatience of the researcher who wants to close the case and stop the thinking from continuing and changing.

2   *Understanding is imaginary* – when the analyst thinks they know exactly what something means, they are most likely to be imposing their own understanding. If relationships between people and the content of their minds was as simple as some humanist psychologists seem to imagine, for example, then it would be possible to produce a clear and transparent understanding of what we all mean. But human experience is more complex than this.

3   *Interpretation unravels symbolic material rather than discloses something under the surface* – the analyst does not search for the real underlying meaning of something, but disturbs the meanings that are already there so that something new can emerge. Crass psychoanalytic psychology tries to find out what the secrets are that are hidden inside people, without realizing that this will throw no light at all on what 'secrecy' itself is and how it gives meaning to what is hidden.

4   *Resistance is on the side of the analyst* – although it is much more convenient to blame the object of the research for being 'resistant' or using other defence mechanisms, it is the analyst's assumptions and actions that are most suspect. Experimental psychologists, for example, are much happier to refer to 'demand characteristics' and 'volunteer traits' as confounding variables in research than to look at how they themselves have set the research up.

5   *There is no metalanguage* – there is no neutral or all-encompassing gods-eye view of things, only commentaries and explanations that are always tied to sets of assumptions and speaking positions. The most bewitching aspect of 'scientific' psychology is the idea that descriptions of what human beings are like and how they work have nothing at all to do with the ideological and political positions of those who are doing the describing.

6   *The real is the impossible* – what is most difficult to bear is that there is no representation of the real that is not always already a representation, and that representation is only part of the picture. 'Cross-cultural' psychology, for example, only makes sense within a certain set of assumptions about the dimensions that the psychology is being compared 'across'. What cross-cultural psychology cannot admit is that 'psychology' itself may not be a dimension other 'cultures' will use.

Psychoanalytic research can help us to reach the parts that other kinds of psychology cannot reach, and its attention to the subjective shape of social phenomena is something that mainstream psychology cannot abide (Malone and Friedlander 2000). It can then be turned explicitly towards action research (Burman 2004a). There are, of course, some dangers in using psychoanalysis. Although it is treated with contempt by experimental psychology, because unconscious processes cannot be predicted and controlled, it is still quite an important part of the psy-complex (Rose 1996). Precisely because psychoanalysis delves deeper into us than other approaches it has often worked as a more efficient and dangerous tool for dividing the normal from the abnormal (Parker *et al.* 1995). What we have to remember when we are using psychoanalysis is that the pathologies that psychoanalysis describes do not lie inside us but in the very process that divides the inside from the outside, so that we then come to imagine that if we look 'inside' individuals we will find the real causes of the things we do.

Further reading

Billig, M. (1999) *Freudian Repression: Conversation Creating the Unconscious.* Cambridge: Cambridge University Press.

Frosh, S. (2002) *After Words: The Personal in Gender, Culture and Psychotherapy.* London: Palgrave.

Hollway, W. (1989) *Subjectivity and Method in Psychology: Gender, Meaning and Science.* London: Sage.

Parker, I. (1997) *Psychoanalytic Culture: Psychoanalytic Discourse in Western Society.* London: Sage.

9   Action research

Action research puts questions of social change on the agenda in every form of qualitative research.

All research is action that works for or against power. The problem with most mainstream psychology is that it either deliberately leaves things as they are – it explicitly reproduces existing power relations – or it pretends that scientific inquiry or interpretation is neutral, and so it gives tacit support to those in power. Qualitative research of all kinds opens the possibility for working 'prefiguratively' – anticipating a better form of society in the very process of struggling for it: 'This combined process of social reform and investigation enables learning about both the freedom of movement to create progressive social forms and about the constraints the present order imposes' (Kagan and Burton 2000: 73). The prefigurative politics that is being argued for here flows from the feminist argument that the personal is political (e.g. Rowbotham *et al.* 1979). An emphasis on the prefigurative aspect of research draws attention to the way that all aspects of our everyday interaction and internal life-world are embedded in social structures, and what happens in the 'personal' sphere is intimately connected with wider patterns of power and resistance.

This attention to the link between the personal and the political may explain both why feminist perspectives have been so important to participatory action research and why feminists have been so interested in making a link between action research and the transformation of psychology (e.g. Brydon-Miller and Tolman 1997). The 'political' aspect of the research then assumes particular importance and 'methods' are then designed to answer research questions in a way that will enable positive political outcomes for those who participate in the research (e.g. Batsleer *et al.* 2002). The emergence of an active tradition of participatory action research in post-apartheid South Africa is an illustration of the way that the political context for research leads to certain questions being asked about the role of the researcher (e.g. Hook *et al.* 2004). This means that radical action research is not a method as such; rather it is *the transformation of research into a prefigurative political practice.*

Such a transformation requires that we grasp the ways in which our research was always from the outset at the very least implicitly political, and that we follow through the ethical and reflexive dimensions of our activity so that the politics becomes explicit to ourselves and to those we work with as our 'co-researchers'.

Four key issues in action research

There are four issues that can facilitate the process of turning the implicit politics of research into something more explicit and transformative.

- First, *the institutional base for our work is always to some extent a hindrance* (even when it could also be something that is a useful resource). Whatever prefigurative project we have in mind, there is already a certain shape to our interactions with potential researchers which is part and parcel of our position in the institution that has made the research possible in the first place. Whether this institution is a university or other place of education, a governmental or non-governmental organization or a private research institute, those we want to work with may have very good reasons not to want to work with us. One way of tackling this is to try to make the university, for example, more accessible (Reason and Bradbury 2001), but this still begs a question about what it is exactly we want to make accessible.

- Second, *the kind of knowledge we produce may not be something that we can 'discover'.* The message that we aim to do 'research' may not be a helpful frame for our activity, and radical action research may lead us to rethink what kind of knowledge we are producing and whether the 'academic research' aspect of it is the least important thing. It may be the case that discovering facts would merely serve to confirm the way things already are rather than change them, and also to confirm the authority of the investigator who managed to find them. There may be good ethical reasons why fictional representation could illustrate ideas more effectively than case studies (Orbach 1999), and in a way that is less intrusive (Rinehart 1998), but only if it did not pretend to rob another of their voice in a false claim to represent them (Khan 1987). (The worked examples in previous chapters analysed material which was fictionalized, based on autobiographical material and discussions with colleagues.)

- Third, *every description we produce or that we encourage our co-researchers to produce is saturated with theory.* What we know is always framed by a range of different contradictory assumptions about the world and what we think will be good for people, and these assumptions are theoretically elaborated. They are not simply mistaken prejudices, but they work because they linked together in complex chains of reasoning and argument. The dictum that there is nothing so practical as a good theory (Lewin 1946) needs to be supplemented by the point that there is nothing so theoretical as a good practice. This does not mean that every theory is correct, and action research is a way of putting theory to the test in practice, and doing this in such a way that those we study are the conscious agents of the research at the same time as they are objects described in the study.

* Fourth, *there is no method that can be applied in action research.* The application of a 'method' in research is always fraught with difficulties, for it presupposes that you can fix what there is that will be of interest to you, and it rules out of consideration that there may be other quite different things that are interesting to those you work with. Instead, you always reinvent method in the process of research (and not only action research), adapting ideas from previous studies and making them useful to the particular topic you are concerned with. And in action research you may not even know what the actual topic is going to be (Granada 1991). If you are really following through your decision to let your co-researchers determine the issues that are relevant to them, then the 'method' itself is likely to be something that will emerge in the course of the research.

Now we can turn to approaches and examples that have worked their way through these issues and are now useful resources for thinking about how we might turn what we do into action research.

Empowerment – pedagogy of the oppressed

Two approaches from two different sites of struggle in the world give some indication as to how the key issues in action research can be linked together.

The first example is from the work of Paulo Freire (1972) who was a Brazilian education activist rooted in the ethos of 'liberation theology', a political movement in the Church that called upon priests to engage in action with the oppressed to fight for a better life on the earth. His work has had a profound impact on participatory action research in Latin America. In Colombia, for example, the Freirian project of 'conscientization' (collective consciousness raising) and 'dialogue' in communities was developed into a full-blown revolutionary project in which social scientists made common cause with radical priests in research projects that were defined by communities for community empowerment (e.g. Fals Borda 1998). The base for this work was often the Church rather than the university, with theology providing the symbolic underpinnings as well as a theory about the nature of evil in the world so that local communities could then invent their own methods for self-education.

The second example comes from Aotearoa where there has been a particular attention to the way that methodologies could be developed in such a way as to 'decolonize' the agendas of the New Zealand government and the dominant white community (Tuhiwai Smith 1999). The focus in this work with indigenous colonized peoples of New Zealand, Australia and the Pacific Islands has taken forward the analyses of 'orientalism' in white western culture (discussed with reference to Edward Said's work in Chapter 4 of this book). This work shows how completely different world views require completely different methodologies, developed from within specific communities, as forms of research that must necessarily aim for change as the research is carried out. Local community education projects are here sometimes connected with the universities, but as independent spaces which draw on stories and theories of the indigenous peoples to 'decolonize methodology'.

There are many other places where research is linked with action and intense practical-theoretical reflection on the forms of 'method' that will take this forward, and in many of the best cases there is no necessary connection between this radical work and psychology (e.g. Desai 2002). These examples of what has been done differently by researchers in other parts of the world are invaluable resources for thinking about how we can make a difference using action research in our own world (and putting the ideas to work in our own academic disciplines).

Box 9.1 *Where are we now with empowerment?*

One of the keywords of action research that serves to draw attention to some of the problems as well as promises of the approach is 'empowerment'. It might be thought of in a number of different senses:

1 *Empowerment as 'helping'* – in which the researcher is charitable to others and gives them a helping hand to do some research.

2 *Empowerment as the task of the 'vanguard'* – in which the researcher leads the oppressed and champions their cause against the oppressors.

3 *Empowerment as 'provocation'* – in which things are stirred up to serve as natural experiments to see what people will do to act on their own behalf.

4 *Empowerment as 'enabling'* – in which research facilitates things to happen without setting the agenda or guiding the activities of co-researchers.

Some of these attempts to 'empower' in the course of research pretend to be very radical, and some of them are worse options than others. The worst option is that psychologists make it part of the disciplinary apparatus to manage their clients (Goodley and Parker 2000).

Radical psychology – application and intervention

One striking example of effective action research in relation to psychiatry in Italy in the 1970s poses important questions for how we sometimes need to do something with knowledge other than research. In Trieste in the north of Italy the old mental hospital San Giovanni was closed and replaced with community mental health centres as part of the mass movement *Psichiatria Democratica* (Parker *et al.* 1995). These events inspired the publication of the 'magazine for democratic psychiatry' *Asylum* in Britain (www.asylumonline.net) and the emergence of a new wave of mental health resistance movements during the 1990s around the 'Hearing Voices Network' (HVN), groups of people who experience what psychiatrists call 'auditory hallucinations' (Blackman 2001).

This network was not based in an academic institution, and the HVN newsletter and *Asylum* magazine always include fiction and poetry, but the links with universities did become a resource for developing new methodologies and new ways of thinking about what 'theory' was. A conference held at Manchester Metropolitan University in 1995, for example, brought together users of psychiatric services, psychiatrists, clinical psychologists, shamans and spiritualists to present and discuss theories about the phenomenon of hearing voices (James 2001). Such an event demanded a rethinking of what the role of discourse analysis should be (McLaughlin 1996) and how psychoanalytic ideas could be adapted and utilized as a form of therapeutic action research (T. McLaughlin 2003). One of the lessons of this movement, which is doing research as part of its political action against the abusive and demeaning practice of psychiatry and psychology, is that old-paradigm quantitative psychological notions of 'testable hypotheses' and 'control groups' will not work in the real world. The movement is mutating so fast, learning from its own experience, that only some of the newer qualitative methods are in any way relevant.

One development since has been the formation of a 'paranoia network' in 2003, and the revival of the 1995 experiment of an academic conference at a university which issues a call for papers and will open up the space of the university to enable challenges to the authority of 'experts' on other people's lives. Involvement in this conference is, of course, 'action research' of some kind, but there are specific questions that the network poses for how we think about the production of knowledge. For example: what would be the role of interviews and observation in a movement that has reason to be suspicious of researchers wanting to know more about them? How might narratives be produced which are creative and illuminating without intruding into experiences that people may want to keep private? When would discursive approaches be helpful or unhelpful as ways to treat the theories the experts and 'experts by experience' (those who actually suffer directly from the effects of psychology) produce as mere discourses rather than claims to truth?

The mental health system survivors movement is but one of the new bases for 'action research' that qualitative psychologists need to look to, and at the very least we need to be able to question our attachment to assumptions about the kind of methods that are dominant in the discipline if we are to make research something relevant to the world outside the universities.

Box 9.2   *Open questions about psychology and liberation*

Latin America has seen a flowering of alternative perspectives and the development of traditions in action research (Montero and Fernández Christlieb 2003), and many researchers there have drawn on 'liberation theology' to turn psychology into 'liberation psychology' (e.g. Martín-Baró 1994). However, rather than jumping too quickly into liberation psychology, perhaps it is better to consider disadvantages to taking debates in theology as our guide.

1   Is this just another opportunity for those with a religious agenda to get a foothold in scientific psychology and turn it into something worse, some other-worldly mysticism, rather than something better?

2   Is there a danger that the power of the priests, shamans and spiritual leaders of different kinds would be reinforced – for those who are already in positions of authority in communities or those who want to make a bid for power?

3   Is there a danger that drawing on theology will also draw in the host of other reactionary ideas that mainstream religions tend to propagate about the role of women and the supposed pathology of certain sexual practices?

Questions of this kind should not only be directed at the role of religious ideas in action research, of course, but at any theoretical system that dogmatically claims to be able to bring the good news or the truth to people: 'We have to recognise the Anglo-Saxon origin of Participant Action Research, as well as its relationship with Protestant methods of indoctrination' (Jiménez-Domínguez 1996: 223).

Participation – recruitment and transformation

Action research could present itself as the most radical version of any other methodology, and so our discussion of action research in this chapter must also temper enthusiasm with some warnings.

There is always a danger that 'interventions' in a community could be just one more effective way of enabling the researcher to come up with the goods. Discussions of community interventions in Colombia, for example, have drawn attention to the way that research by followers of Freire coexists with 'interventions' by evangelical churches, ecological groups, private companies, universities and the army (Granada 1991). All of these different interventions are in one way or another 'action research', some very unpleasant and dangerous.

There is a danger that the researcher may be so besotted by the struggle of the people against reactionary institutions – which are often perceived to include universities – that they dissolve their research agenda into a simplistic celebration of the knowledge of the people. Action research in Colombia, inspired by Freire and then taken in an even more radical direction by Orlando Fals Borda, followed this route for some time (Jiménez-Domínguez 1996).

There is a danger that 'participation' will be assumed to be a good thing, and the researcher will lose sight of the way that local communities, resistance movements, and self-help groups may have very good reasons to avoid participating. Discussions of the recruitment into research as a 'new tyranny', particularly in relation to parts of the world that are dependent on the goodwill of the imperialist nations, have shown how well-meaning academics may end up disempowering people at the very moment that they claim to promise participation and empowerment (Cooke and Kothari 2001).

Each of these dangers illustrates the importance of attending to the way that the apparent absence of power in a community or a research relationship may actually be obscuring all the more efficiently the privilege certain people have to speak and determine what is to be done. The most 'open' organization may be afflicted by a 'tyranny of structurelessness' in which there is the pretence that everything is fine and that anyone who complains has a problem (Freeman 1996).

Box 9.3 *Explicating the parameters of action research*

It is easier to say what action research is not than what it is, and it is worth being aware of issues that will lead you astray. Attending to these temptations should serve as guidelines for developing your own practice in action research more effectively than telling you directly what you must do.

---

1 *Do not treat it as a method of research* – if action research is described as a 'method' you will actually end up with an eclectic mixture in which it will be more difficult to identify conceptual and political problems, and advantages of radical approaches and existing methods.

2 *Do not commit yourself to following through one method* – if action research is tied to one particular course of action it will render impossible creative ways of thinking about how methods may emerge as the study is developed collaboratively with co-researchers.

3 *Do not pretend that there is only action* – there is always a structured set of relations between researcher and researched, and between researcher and those they report to, and a refusal to acknowledge these relations can merely serve to obscure the 'tyranny of structurelessness'.

4 *Do not think that you will be successful if you are nice* – even the most collaborative and open action research involves argument and conflict over different perspectives and interests, and it is better to focus on these points of antagonism than to pretend that they can be smoothed over.

Politics – academic frames and their outside

Action research may be a good way of finding out things, but in some cases it may be most effective when it gives up on the aim of producing 'knowledge' and focuses instead on the way that knowledge is produced (Holzman 1999). The decisions that the researcher then takes about whether they are going to produce knowledge, and who it should be for, will be ethical decisions. However, the ethos of action research is such that the ethical choices are collectively made – with the co-researchers rather than hidden away in the office of the academic – and so the ethics become more closely bound up with politics. And the collective nature of these decisions means that the reflexive engagement of the researcher is all the more intense. The discussions of the theoretical grounding of our research and ethical and reflexive dimensions of research practice (discussed in the first three chapters of this book) are taken further by debates in action research.

The political aspect of research – political in the sense of day-to-day interactions and relationships that are woven into broader patterns of power and resistance – is also evident when we try to evaluate action research, and any appeal to fixed 'criteria' may end up invalidating the work. We need to find a way of developing criteria that will respect the contribution of 'experts by experience' and the way that the 'method' in a study may only emerge through cooperation with these kinds of expert (e.g. Bracken and Thomas 2001). The role of the academic frame in our work also, of course, has consequences for the way we write reports about what we have done. The attempt to fix on any particular method, or to treat action research as if it were a method and relentlessly 'apply' it regardless of what is happening in the course of the work, is one of the ways that traditional academic practice in psychology makes radical research more difficult (Duckett and Pratt 2001). (I have tried to keep these issues in mind in the discussion of criteria and reporting in the final two chapters of the book.)

Box 9.4 *Don't stop there! Beyond action research*

Action research borrows ideas from outside academic institutions, and it would indeed be a betrayal of the ethos of this approach to then isolate it and cut its links with the traditions of work it is indebted to.

1 *Feminist politics* – the emphasis on working prefiguratively emerged from the women's movement, specifically from debates in socialist feminism, and the gender dimension inside and outside research institutions can too easily fade into the background when men take over and lead action research projects.

2 *Anti-racist politics* – dominant cultural agendas are often quite apparent in mainstream psychology, but it is worth bearing in mind that different forms of action research are also closely tied to the history of colonialism, and that 'action' in research may be oppressive rather than liberating.

3 *Class politics* – the notion of prefigurative action research has a two-way link with the way we engage in political change, and this includes the way we develop theoretical language as a form of jargon which reproduces the privileged relationship between intellectual and manual labour.

4 *Academic politics* – research often leads people inside academic, governmental and private institutions to think only in terms of job security and their next career move, but action research should be developed in relation to the agendas of those who are usually excluded from these institutions.

Qualitative research in psychology opens a space for turning mere academic investigation into prefigurative political practice, for turning qualitative psychology into something that is challenging and transformative.

Any 'method' in qualitative psychology can be developed into action research, but some of the methods discussed in this book are more immediately suited to action research than others.

Psychoanalysis, for example, is often too easily used as a tool to diagnose and interpret others, and some work needs to be done to make it accessible to people rather than simply be 'applied' to them (Burman 2004a). Even then, that very accessibility may encourage more people outside psychology to mystify their friends and themselves when they start using its peculiar jargon. One way of tackling that problem is to treat psychoanalytic jargon as one powerful discourse that circulates in western culture, and discourse research can enable us to step back from psychology and treat the accounts given by psychologists as discourses rather than facts about behaviour and experience that normalize things that are acceptable and that pathologize people who do not fit in (e.g. Parker 2004b). Discourse analysis may then be turned into a form of action research when it encourages people to make links between language, power and resistance (e.g. Burman *et al.* 1996). Even then, the focus on language may sidetrack people from the more pressing material aspects of oppression and political action.

Narrative approaches make a more direct connection between language and experience than many discourse-analytic studies have done, and there is already a political movement inspired by theoretical discussions of the performance of identity in narrative; queer theory and queer politics have shown how the narratives we tell about ourselves can be turned into action (e.g. Watson forthcoming). Even then, the claim that identity is simply an effect of a narrative may make it more difficult for those who want to insist that they really have discovered their real identity as a member of a particular community. Ethnography is, in this respect, a good corrective, for it has the potential to enable members of a community to question the ways in which they are coerced into adopting a certain identity and into saying that they really correspond to it. Ethnographic research that focuses on processes of inclusion, exclusion and power can then become a form of action research (e.g. Evans 2002). Even then, an ethnography that does not directly involve people in the work as co-researchers still gives the point of view of an 'outsider' who observes and comments upon others. This is why interviewing has been so appealing to radical qualitative researchers, and when there is a link with action research it becomes possible to involve participants in a reflexive cycle of accounting and action (e.g. Pratt *et al.* 2004).

Even then, each approach is still framed by the imperative to produce an academic product, and only a political critique of the discipline of psychology which is part of an apparatus of control and individualization under capitalism will enable us to step back, to step outside the frame of academic work and to do something more effective (e.g., Melancholic Troglodytes 2003). The personal stake we have in psychological investigations may then really be transformed into genuinely political 'action research'.

Further reading

Brydon-Miller, M. and Tolman, D.L. (eds) (1997) Transforming psychology: interpretive and participatory research methods (special issue), *Journal of Social Issues*, 53(4).

Cooke, B. and Kothari, U. (eds) (2001) *Participation: The New Tyranny?* London: Zed Books.

Melancholic Troglodytes (eds) (2003) Anti-capitalism (special issue), *Annual Review of Critical Psychology*, 3.

10 Criteria

Qualitative research in psychology poses questions about the nature of 'criteria' that need to be reflexively embedded in any alternative guidelines. Two problems with fixed 'criteria' should be noted. First, most traditional quantitative psychological research does not adhere to the criteria it desires, and in many cases it would be very difficult to insist that it does. Some of the most innovative studies in quantitative research have broken the rules of accepted scientific inquiry, and it has been through awareness that something radically different was being undertaken and an argument for what was new that progress has been possible (Salmon 2003). It would be reasonable to ask that quantitative research should also justify itself against the issues raised here. Second, criteria of any kind risk legitimating certain varieties of qualitative research, marginalizing others, and so stifling new methodological developments (Elliott *et al.* 1999). That is why I explicate some parameters for research and emphasize that the key question that the researcher should explicate for themselves, and perhaps even indicate to their readers, is 'by what should I be judged?'

An appeal to different distinctive criteria is one way of warranting the range of innovative ways of going about research. For students the criteria elaborated in this chapter will draw attention to issues that they might consider as they formulate their research and prepare it for evaluation. For supervisors these guidelines could serve to provide enough common ground between psychologists carrying out qualitative or quantitative research, but this common ground can only be secured on the understanding that some flexibility and negotiation is needed so that both students and supervisors can formulate their own particular procedures for describing, explaining and justifying what they have done. So, the criteria for good research are *guidelines that are closed enough to guide evaluation and open enough to enable transformation of assumptions*.

These descriptions of 'criteria', then, should be read as flexible guidelines or touchstones, and they are made as explicit as possible here as part of the process of making transparent the reasons and ways we go about doing research and the reasons and ways we judge, and ask others to judge, its value.

Four key issues in the formulation of criteria

The process of making research questions and their evaluation transparent within (and beyond) the psychological community and exploring what they may mean is more important here than fixing meanings and then refusing reinterpretation. Accordingly, there are four key issues that qualitative researchers in psychology need to address.

- The first is an awareness of *the difference between qualitative approaches and traditional quantitative research*. There are historical divisions between the two approaches, and this has led to the supervision of undergraduate qualitative research to become a sometimes marginalized speciality, with recommendations put forward as to which particular methods might be easier to incorporate in teaching in the discipline (e.g. Gough *et al.* 2003). There is also a history of argument over the 'paradigm' that should govern psychological research (Harré 2004), an issue covered in Box 10.1.

- Second, there is a range of resources qualitative researchers have drawn upon to develop alternative methods. *Some of the most valuable of these are outside the discipline.* Feminist debates about how we produce knowledge have been crucial to radical reflections on science, and have huge consequences for qualitative research (e.g. Hartsock 1987). Qualitative research outside psychology, the best of which has been heavily influenced by feminism, has also led to different varieties of 'constructionist' criteria that challenge mainstream psychology (e.g. Denzin and Lincoln 2000).

- The third issue is explicit consideration of the way criteria should be understood in a particular case. *There is no overall set of criteria that would work to justify a specific study*, for a new research question calls for a new rationale and combination of methodological resources to explore it, and the terms in which a research question is framed will entail particular methods. The best research entails an innovation not only with respect to the topic but also with respect to the methodology that will be appropriate to address it. The problem of how to legitimize existing research cannot be solved by constructing an iron grid that will thereby invalidate all the new things that will be developed later on (Capdevila 2003).

- Fourth, there is a requirement that the researcher gives an account of the ways in which *the research relates specifically to psychology*. The problem that needs to be grasped here is that psychology as a discipline has historically defined itself with reference to methodology more than by the objects or topics of research (Rose 1985).

Now it is necessary to find a way to open up new ways of thinking about the domain of the 'psychological' – perhaps by refocusing on such things as 'experience', 'subjectivity' or 'interaction' – so that the methodologies we develop follow from the research question.

This chapter addresses those four issues in relation to how we might think about the 'criteria' for good research.

Paradigmatic framing – options and exclusions

It is worthwhile reminding ourselves about some of the ways in which assumptions that underpin quantitative research are inappropriate to qualitative studies. This is not at all to say that qualitative researchers are uninterested in quantitative research. In fact, the questioning of assumptions that underpins much quantitative psychology has been going on in the field of social statistics for many years (e.g. Dorling and Simpson 1999) and some of us would like to see good quantitative research in psychology take these debates on board. There are three main issues here.

First, it is possible to see 'objectivity' as something that is constructed, sometimes for very good reasons. This construction of objectivity does not mean that some views of the world are better than others, but it does mean that we cannot take a seemingly objective account for granted. The most important issue here is that with respect to psychological research, the person carrying out the research always has a certain stance toward the questions that are being explored. Hunches, intuitions, hopes and assumptions about the nature of human beings all play a role in the apparently 'objective' pursuit of a psychologist. This position – whether as empathic involvement or studied detachment – is a form of subjectivity (Hollway 1989). This is why qualitative researchers often prefer to work with subjectivity rather than against it (which is what we take quantitative researchers often to be doing when they say they are being objective).

Second, qualitative researchers see 'validity' as resting on a mistaken view that different ways of representing phenomena will necessarily be representing the same thing. It is all the more the case with psychological research that the particular standpoint we have towards other people, and what we expect them to be like, will make every description we give open to challenge. The claim that qualitative researchers are describing the 'same thing' is to close down the possible alternative ways of describing experience, even leaving aside for the moment the difficult question as to whether we should simply respect the accounts that someone gives of their own experience or whether the reasons people do things can be made transparent to the researcher (Nightingale and Cromby 1999). This is why qualitative researchers often prefer to explore the various different ways of describing an issue.

Third, traditionally 'reliability' is seen as taking for granted that our objects of study remain stable over time rather than being liable to change. This is an assumption underlying conceptions of method in psychology that is closely linked to deeper assumptions about the importance of 'consistency' and 'rationality' in western psychology. But some forms of research, action research, make that process of change the very topic that is focused upon, and there is an explicit attempt to make sure that things do not stay the same (Kagan and Burton 2000). The lesson of community empowerment work and 'prefigurative' action research for psychology is not so much that change can occur, but that it is happening all the time. This is why good qualitative research often focuses on change and traces a process, rather than treating patterns of human behaviour or thinking as things that are fixed.

These perspectives on 'objectivity', 'validity' and 'reliability' of course raise questions for the kind of positivist science that has been popular with psychologists because they make it seem as if stable facts about people can be accumulated and then taken for granted for further study by an objective researcher.

Box 10.1 *Where are we now with science?*

Psychologists sometimes argue that only quantitative research is properly 'scientific', or that qualitative research should be evaluated against the kind of criteria that have usually been employed to assess quantitative research. However, these arguments can just as well be turned around to put the quantitative researchers on the spot. The philosopher of science Rom Harré (2004), for example, argues that it is *qualitative* research that is properly scientific, and that it is only in relation to methodological debates in that strand of work that we can start to explore how quantitative research might measure up to it. The relevant elements of Harré's argument are the following.

1 *Reflexivity* – the particular object of study for any science needs to be carefully specified. Qualitative research takes seriously a crucial aspect of the nature of its object of study: human action and experience. The human being is able to reflect on its behaviour and to engage in second-level reflection on those reflections. This is why the reflexive work of the researcher is also a crucial part of any genuine scientific study.

2 *Meaning* – the nature of the material that is studied by a science needs to be understood. Qualitative research focuses on the way in which meaningful qualities of human 'experience' or 'subjectivity'

are represented to others. The accounts that people give for what they do may or may not correspond to what they actually think about those things. But the 'discovery' or 'production' of meaning is a necessary aspect of the scientific study of human psychology.

3   *Specificity* – the level of analysis and the claims that are made from work in a particular domain need to be clearly spelt out. Qualitative research often engages in intensive case studies that are not directly extrapolated to populations, or in studies of collective activity that are not directly extrapolated to individual members. The scientific task in this work is to account for the specific nature and limits of the account, and for what may be learnt from it.

The old laboratory-experimental 'paradigm' of research in psychology was, Harré argues, 'pre-scientific', and the task that *quantitative* researchers face now is how to account for the reflexive capacity of human beings, the meaningful nature of the data they produce and the way that claims are made about individuals from aggregated descriptions of behaviour from particular populations. There are some possibilities of very good innovative research in this tradition that addresses itself to these issues and to the guidelines outlined in this chapter.

Conceptual resources – handled with care

Some of the conceptual resources qualitative researchers have used will be appropriate for future research, but we also need to take into account the particular ways in which they may be helpful or unhelpful depending on each study. These resources do not of themselves solve problems in research. Rather, qualitative researchers take them seriously because of the additional fruitful questions they raise.

First, the claim to be 'neutral' in research is one that sustains a particular standpoint and to prevent the standpoint from being opened to question. In contrast, a qualitative researcher may address subjectivity, exploring emotional investments in the topic, focusing on the position of the researcher and making our moral-political standpoint clear (Wilkinson 1988). A reflexive analysis in a report can serve to help the reader understand something more about the work. This is sometimes included in the report as one of the subsections of the 'analysis' and marked as 'reflexive analysis', or put in the discussion as part of a reflection on the process of carrying out the research (or both). This is the place to consider the passionate interests that drive some of the best research (Maso 2003). However, this attempt to question the ostensible neutrality of the research can be tackled in what some might see as 'confessional' mode (in which there is a story about the researcher's journey into the research and how they felt about it), but it may also be tackled by giving an account of the institutional background for the formulation and representation of what the research is about. That is, the 'position of the researcher' is a question of institutional reflexivity that draws attention to how this research is being carried out and in whose interests.

Second, qualitative research has opened up a series of questions about the participation of those who are studied and whether they are treated as mere objects by traditional psychological research. The key question here is how the different positions that are brought to bear on the research throw new light on key issues. We might ask our co-researchers (our 'subjects') to respond to the analysis, and this may be with the aim of securing respondent validation (to confirm certain interpretations) or to encourage disagreement (and to raise alternative interpretations). These options, however morally compelling, cannot apply to all kinds of qualitative research, especially where the analysis of meaning does not aim to privilege the immediate perspective of the speaker (Kitzinger and Wilkinson 1997). Most forms of discourse analysis, for example, need to clarify why it would not be appropriate to add further accounts to the layers of interpretation they have constructed in their readings of the texts (Burman 2004b).

Third, however tempting it is to claim that the research has provided a clearer or more superior view of what is going on, we need to hesitate a moment and explore what grounds we have for that claim. We may use a variety of different methods that help us to 'triangulate' our inquiry, and qualitative researchers may do this to show the different ways in which an issue might be understood. This may either be with the aim of arriving at a common view or alternatively to illustrate the intrinsic complexity of the issue (Tindall 1994). If there were really a definitive explanation then the assessment of research would be quite simple, and would revolve around the brutal question as to whether the researcher has got it right or wrong (in which case they pass or fail the evaluation). Processes of 'triangulation' of research, however, are better used in such a way that alternative explanations may coexist, and then the question to be addressed by the researcher is how their own particular interpretations can be justified and what the consequences would be of taking them seriously.

These questions about 'neutrality', 'confirmation' of findings and the idea that there is a 'definitive' account draw attention to the contested nature of qualitative research. What this 'quality' amounts to is a question of debate, as we note in Box 10.2.

Box 10.2 *Open questions about quality*

It is crucial to the enterprise of scientific work generally, and qualitative research in particular, that the way we go about it is open to debate. Here are some questions for which there are no clear answers and much disagreement.

1   *What counts as good?* (a) It corresponds to the norms of established scientific study. (b) It will improve the lives of those who participated. (c) It is intrinsically interesting and will provoke and satisfy those who are curious about the questions posed.

2   *Who should it be for?* (a) It should be directly accessible to ordinary people outside psychology. (b) It should contribute to the accumulating body of knowledge for the use of other researchers. (c) Those who participated should gain something from it in exchange for their time.

3   *What counts as analysis?* (a) A careful redescription using some categories from a particular framework. (b) The discovery of something that can be empirically confirmed as true or refused as false. (c) The emergence of a new meaning that was entirely unexpected.

4   *What is the role of theory?* (a) Mystification by those versed in jargon at the expense of those who participated. (b) A necessary antidote to the common-sense and often mistaken explanations for human behaviour. (c) The space for thinking afresh about something.

This is not a multiple-choice test (which, of course, would be a most inappropriate assessment for qualitative research). These open questions are puzzles for us and for our colleagues, and good research puzzles about them a bit further and positions itself in relation to them.

Guidelines – the rules and the exceptions

Three overarching criteria for good research can be identified, but we need these to be able to operate in ways that are not fixed in stone (that is, they may be reflexively employed or challenged depending on the kind of study). In each case, then, we should value each criteria *and* each exception.

First, with respect to the *grounding* of the work in existing research, this means that the work should identify existing lines of research around the issue and locate itself, *but* there may be cases when absences in the research literature are important and so the research will have to address these (e.g. Phoenix 1994). If it were not possible to identify an absence and explore why that were so, no new objects of psychological research would ever appear.

Second, with respect to *coherence* in the argument of the study, this means that there could be a cumulative linear narrative which moves clearly from point to point to arrive at conclusions, *but* there may be cases where a more deliberately open and fragmented narrative will be more appropriate (e.g. Curt 1994). The standard format of a research report is a secure framework for many writers, but it is itself a particular genre of writing that can turn into a constraint and inhibit innovative work.

Third, with respect to the *accessibility* of presentation, clearly accounting for the conceptual background, research process and new perspectives (which may include accounts, knowledge, interpretations) are important. We may also want the work to be accessible to those outside the research community, *but* there may be times when difficult arguments make difficult reading. With respect to each of these, the study should make clear by what kinds of rules it should be evaluated, and warrant the following or breaking of these rules. This is an issue that connects with the common-sense views of the self that circulate in psychology, views that may only be opened up for study by refusing to speak those descriptions of ourselves that everyone takes for granted (Terre Blanche and Durrheim 1999).

The questions in Box 10.3, which explicates the 'parameters of criteria', are designed to draw attention to assumptions about research that usually govern quantitative research in psychology, but these mainstream assumptions are placed 'under erasure'. They are marked in this way precisely to remind you that any ~~checklist~~ always need to be challenged as such if the guidelines are to be flexible enough to leave space for innovations in research practice.

Box 10.3 *Explicating the parameters of criteria*

These points summarize key questions that should be considered in the process of carrying out qualitative research in psychology.

1 ~~Objective?~~ – have you described what theoretical resources you draw upon to make your subjectivity into a useful device and how those resources impact on the research?

2 ~~Valid?~~ – have you made clear the ways in which the account you give is distinctive and paradigmatically different from other things that might be categorized along with it?

3 ~~Reliable?~~ – have you traced a process of change in your understanding and other people's understanding of the topic and explored how views of it may continue to change?

4 ~~Neutral?~~ – is there a reflexive analysis which steps back from the account you have given and allows the reader to see something of the institutional vantage point from which the story is told?

5 ~~Confirmed?~~ – is there an attempt to bring research participants' responses to the analysis into the study, and an attempt both to clarify the ways in which they agree and disagree with what you say and to analyse why and how these different responses may have come about?

6 ~~Definitive?~~ – is there an attempt to 'triangulate' views of the topic and a decision about whether this triangulation should be taken as arriving at a clearer view or an explication of what is apparent from different vantage points?

7 ~~Established?~~ – if you did not study and refer to an established line of research, did you discuss the reasons why this may not appear in the research literature?

8 ~~Coherent?~~ – if you did not organize your material in a coherent way, did you say why you chose a different kind of narrative to display your research and thus persuade the reader that this work is worthwhile?

9 ~~Accessible?~~ – if you did not arrive at something that could be easily accessible to someone in the discipline or outside it, did you say why your work needed to be more complex?

10 ~~Psychological?~~ – have you made clear that the theoretical or methodological framework you have used is from within the domain of psychology, or made clear how the topic is usually understood by psychology, or examined what the implications of what you have done might be for psychology?

Psychological questions – including questioning psychology

Qualitative research is sometimes opposed by quantitatively-inclined assessors in the discipline on the grounds that it is not 'really' psychology. This objection to qualitative research is sometimes raised alongside the argument that psychology should be a 'science' (a topic addressed in Box 10.1). This opposition between science and non-science used by some quantitative psychologists tends to reinforce an unnecessarily firm distinction between quantitative and qualitative approaches, a distinction that has itself been challenged by the most innovative research in psychology over the years. We need to remember that many kinds of research in psychology have developed through interdisciplinary work which has disturbed the boundaries between the discipline of psychology and other disciplines, and that research in other countries which is carried out in psychology departments often draws on a range of different theoretical frameworks and methodological approaches. Broadly speaking, though, qualitative research may defend its place in the discipline on one or more of the following grounds.

First, the theory used or challenged in the study may be from within psychology. Here we would expect that the theories concerned are outlined and referenced so that a judgement can be made of the pertinence of the critique to the study. Second, the topic being explored or reframed may usually be included within the domain of psychology. Here we would expect an outline of the relevant literature on the topic and some questions to be raised about that literature that pave the way for the particular research questions in the study. Third, the fact that there are psychological implications of the research should be clearly stated at the outset. Here we may expect that the relevant issues concerning 'psychology', 'experience' or 'subjectivity' are outlined and the consequences of adopting one or other of these descriptive terms explored.

Three core principles are worth bearing in mind as we orientate ourselves toward good research in psychology that is able to encompass work sceptical about the underlying assumptions that psychologists usually make about what counts as good research. These principles, outlined by qualitative researchers in the discipline who have helped to push the limits of what was acceptable under the old 'laboratory-experimental' paradigm, help set out a way of thinking about how supervisors might facilitate and evaluate student work.

The first is that of 'apprenticeship'. This notion draws attention to the way that students learn to speak the language of the particular discipline or craft they are learning, and how they set out any innovations against the background of those existing practices. Qualitative work does not at all mean disregarding or throwing away the knowledge that has been accumulated by psychology. The question is how the researcher positions themselves against that knowledge. To put the point at its most extreme, and for those who really have concluded that this knowledge is useless, we still expect that the sceptic will be able to weave an impression of excellence. Unthinkingly reproducing the language of the discipline regardless of the research paradigm that has been adopted is an error (Burman 1998b).

The second principle is that of 'scholarship'. We encourage the student to be immersed in the relevant debates so that they are able to make an argument for what they find to be valuable or unsatisfactory about them. A degree of rhetorical, sometimes polemical, skill is required in order to construct an argument that both marshals evidence and steers a course through debates in order to persuade the reader. To put this point at its most extreme, and for those who feel passionately that what psychology says is wrong, we still expect that this opponent of mainstream psychology is able to find some grounds from which they can reason with their audience. All good scientific research is driven by a passion to explore particular questions and to persuade others of a point of view (Billig 1988).

The third principle concerns 'innovation'. There is a corresponding danger here of 'methodolatry', which is that the way in which the research is designed and carried out takes precedence and the actual research question gets lost. It may indeed be the case that a particular methodology becomes the topic of the research, but even in this case there is a research question (which focuses on the way something is investigated). To put this point in the most extreme way, for those who do want to break all the rules about methodology that they have learned in the discipline, we still expect that this anarchic position is able to show that it knows very well what it is pitting itself against so that it does not let those who simply repeat the tried and tested rules of research off the hook. Those who have simply refused the rules of method without careful argument for the position they take, and why, are all the more likely to fall foul of 'methodolatry' (Reicher 2000). These three principles are summed up in Box 10.4.

Box 10.4 *Don't stop there! Beyond criteria*

The best research goes beyond even these criteria to open up something new, so that the work is innovative not only with respect to the content of the study (what has been studied and what has been discovered) but also with respect to its form (how the research questions were explored and how they were interpreted). Three watchwords for opening the way to the best research are:

1 *Apprenticeship* – the ability to use existing resources and position oneself within or in relation to a certain tradition of work. A good competent research report (for a lower second class or 'C' grade) is one that displays an understanding of the key issues outlined in this chapter and which has thought through the specific questions that the guidelines raise.

2 *Scholarship* – showing that some underlying premises and assumptions in existing relevant studies have been grasped. A very good research report (for an upper second class or 'B' grade) is one that brings that understanding to bear in order to construct an argument, perhaps polemical, against the limits of methodological procedures that may inhibit new ways of doing research.

> 3 *Innovation* – producing work that may transform the coordinates
> by which a problem is usually understood. An excellent research
> report (for a first class or 'A' grade) is one that 'discovers' or
> 'produces' something new and which is able to reflexively embed
> its account of what has happened within and against usual taken-
> for-granted practices in research.
>
> Use the guidelines in so far as they help, but if necessary challenge the
> ground rules that we have used to formulate them!

This chapter covers the terrain over which qualitative researchers in psychology may have to travel, and its aim is not so much to be prescriptive as to clearly outline the range of issues that researchers (whether qualitative or quantitative) need to tackle. The chapter focuses on psychology, but also has strong affinity with debates in qualitative evaluation produced by the National Health Service Research and Development Programme (Murphy *et al.* 1998) and for the Cabinet Office (Spencer *et al.* 2003). It is important for researchers to bear these issues in mind when, for example, they do or do not formulate 'hypotheses' before they carry out their study, when they do or do not follow a series of methodological steps, or when they do or do not separate analysis from discussion in the written report. Quantitative researchers all too often follow well-established procedures without reflecting on what they are doing and why. We should not encourage qualitative researchers to make the same mistake. Qualitative research often seems more difficult because it requires a higher level of reflection and accountability (to oneself, to colleagues and to others), and this is why an apparently simple issue like 'criteria' involves some sustained conceptual work that should then find its way into the writing of the report.

Further reading

Curt, B.C. (1994) *Textuality and Tectonics: Troubling Social and Psychological Science*. Buckingham: Open University Press.

Hartsock, N. (1987) The feminist standpoint: developing the ground for a specifically feminist historical materialism, in S. Harding (ed.) *Feminism and Methodology: Social Science Issues*. Bloomington, IN: Indiana University Press.

Salmon, P. (2003) How do we recognise good research? *The Psychologist*, 16(1): 24–7.

11 Reporting

Good qualitative research reports in psychology must weave themselves around the limits imposed on good writing in the discipline.

A report written in the style of 'old paradigm' laboratory-experimental psychology pretends to give the bare facts about existing research on a topic and the methodology that will be employed. The writer hides behind an impersonal writing style – third-person reports which are careful never to reveal anything of their own standpoint – and we learn little about the actual interaction that took place with those who were involved in the study. And the rigid format of the report – Introduction, Method, Results and Discussion – reflects the assumptions many quantitative psychologists make about the importance of neutral 'scientific' language to describe what they think they have discovered. The format and language of most quantitative psychology makes for dull and bad writing. The first timid step we take over the limits to good writing in qualitative research, then, is to modify the contents list of the report, so that the 'Results' are replaced with 'Analysis'.

There are no 'results' in qualitative research, and we should remember that 'analysis' is a series of interpretations that are open to question. The best report helps the reader to open up new questions about what they have been told. The shift into radical research writing then comes about as we follow through the consequences of turning the results into analysis so that we are then able to make our interpretations and discussion into something creative, enjoyable to read and illuminating. This means that the issue opened up in the introduction and teased through in the analysis and discussion should locate the author as an ethical reflexive agent in the research and connect the work with references so that the reader can also locate themselves in it if they want to take it further. The reporting of a piece of research should be a way of *conveying to the reader some new perspectives and some resources for them to take the research forward*.

This chapter traces through some of the ethical reflexive choices that the researcher needs to make about how they represent what they have done and the ways in which the structure of the report can be used to convey something surprising to its different kinds of reader.

Four key issues in writing reports

Some of the most intensely reflexive work on writing as a particular form of representation was carried out by the historian and philosopher Michel Foucault (whose work was briefly discussed in Chapter 1). His research on discipline and confession in western society underpins crucial discussions of 'reflexivity' in the modern human sciences. Although he trained as a psychologist himself, it would seem odd to many of his readers today to use his work to guide us as to how we might produce qualitative psychology research reports. However, in his inaugural lecture at the Collège de France he drew attention to characteristics of writing that are relevant now to how we write (Foucault 1970). In that lecture he set out four methodological requirements to the work he wanted to carry out and their consequences. I will elaborate on these here in relation to qualitative research.

- First is the principle of *reversal*. Foucault set himself against 'the author, the discipline, the will to truth' (1970: 67) as principles that limit the way we think about things. Instead of justifying a piece of research because it is following faithfully in the tracks of another great psychologist (the 'author'), because it is a recognized research topic in psychology (the 'discipline') or because it is accumulating knowledge about something just for the sake of it (the 'will to truth'), we need to reverse things so that we throw existing research into question. How do certain ways of cutting up the world mislead and reflect the assumptions of certain authors and research traditions, and how could we think about a topic in a different way and study it in such a way that even its status as something essentially psychological might be challenged? This is a task for the introduction of a report where existing 'authorities' are cited and alternative ways of looking at the topic are set out.
- Second is the principle of *exteriority*. Rather than pretend that we can delve inside and underneath things to explain why something happens, Foucault urged us to 'go towards its external conditions of possibility, towards what gives rise to the aleatory [random] series of these events, and fixes its limits' (Foucault 1970: 67). The question we always need to ask about existing research is how it might have come about that psychologists described a particular phenomenon in the way they did, what the 'conditions of possibility' were that enabled them to describe things in a certain way. The key task of an Introduction is to examine how certain kinds of explanation function and how certain limits are set in place by those explanations. It is then possible to look at alternative ways of exploring a topic, and a task for the review of methodology in the

Introduction section to the report, and for the outline of what is to be done the Method section, is to outline ways of examining the topic in such a way as to open up alternative accounts rather than shut things down.

- Third is the principle of *specificity*. Here Foucault was concerned with overarching accounts, and the way that these function to obscure and exclude the things that do not fit; this is 'a violence which we do to things' (1970: 67). The best research in the discipline has always valued the particular strange things that human beings do, and looked to the idiosyncratic out-of-the-ordinary ways that people cope to give some insight into how psychology is continually transforming itself to meet new challenges. Some of the best research now included in all standard psychology textbooks actually had no 'hypotheses' and was rejected by journals because it was written in a way that drew attention to something new. The task now is to resist the temptation to treat that innovative work as if it 'discovered' the truth about human behaviour, and the Introduction, Method and Analysis sections of a report needs to set out 'research questions' that are open to the possibility that something surprising might happen and that something interesting might be suggested.

- Fourth is the principle of *discontinuity*. Rather than trying to tie all the threads together into a cover-all explanation for a phenomenon or attempting to discover something under the surface that will explain away all the contradictory versions of a phenomenon, Foucault aimed to highlight 'discontinuous practices, which cross each other, are sometimes juxtaposed with one another, but can just as well exclude or be unaware of each other' (Foucault 1970: 67). Psychology as a discipline all too often reduces the variety of accounts that people give of their experiences to behavioural patterns or underlying cognitive processes or wired-in biological 'human nature'. Good qualitative research questions this pervasive reductionism. This is a task for the Analysis and Discussion, where different possible interpretations are offered and there is some consideration of what the implications of the different interpretations are.

Foucault's discussion of how to carry out research is yet another powerful example of why we need theory to help us reflect on how we produce empirical work and how we write it up. We can now go further with these key reflexive issues about writing and turn to *who* we write for.

Accounting (with the audience in mind)

Mainstream researchers in psychology have tended to grab the data and run as far away from their 'subjects' as possible, being careful only to promise very long-term, indirect benefits to those who have taken part in a study (or to deny any responsibility for bad things that happen to co-researchers because they have signed 'consent'). The process of writing the report has then tended to be just as ethically problematic, with assessment panels and funding bodies served up as much information as they want in whatever format they the would like it. Qualitative researchers – radical or not – have to steer their way through exactly the same kind of expectations from readers, whether they are based in academic, community, governmental or private organizations.

However flexible the criteria are for assessing the work, there are ethical compromises that have to be made when the report is written. (Here we take forward some of the issues that were raised in Chapter 2, on ethics in research.)

We can consider the act of carrying out research as an 'event' that places the researcher in a peculiar position when they come to report what they have done to someone else (cf. Badiou 2001). Now we are faced with an ethical choice, as to how we maintain our fidelity to that event and how we betray it. This is particularly important when the research involves other people, those we prefer now to call our 'co-researchers'. Certain promises about anonymity need to be honoured, and you need to be clear with them, and with the reader, about the difference between anonymity (that the reader will not be able to identify those who took part) and confidentiality (a promise that is almost always impossible to honour, for the very reason that other people outside the research relationship will be reading and assessing the work). In some cases the ethical choice may be even more acute, for it is quite possible that the co-researchers wanted to be named (and then the research report guarantees neither confidentiality nor anonymity). Fidelity to the event that is the act of research can only be carried forward into the writing if co-researchers are genuinely and meaningfully able to determine the content of a report, and this is only possible if the process of writing is discussed with them from the start.

The problem is compounded if we bring the expectations of the readers into the equation, for they will want to know exactly what has been done with whom, and what was found. You agreed to carry out a piece of research knowing that you were going to write a report, and you know that you have to present what you have done in a certain format in order to meet certain institutional requirements. The relationship with those in the institution who are assessing the work therefore also poses a question about fidelity and betrayal. There are ways through this, but they do not enable us to escape the ethical dimension of managing the competing sets of relationships. One best way is to write as closely as possible to the format that is demanded by assessors in the institution you are based in – to weave an impression of excellence (cf. Curt 1994) – but to be open about the ethical distance you need to do this in two arenas: in the relationships you maintain with your co-researchers (do not close down your contact with them when the research is over) and in the space for reflexive analysis that qualitative research reports now permit. There is more on this space in the next section of this chapter.

The task is not to avoid these problems but to be aware of how they will always structure the way a report is written, who it will please and why.

Box 11.1 *Where are we now with accessibility?*

Academic and professional language is a peculiar closed system, a way of describing the world that is very different from everyday 'common sense'. Every theoretical framework in psychology comprises new terminology or words that are used very differently from the meanings they have in the outside 'real world'. What are the consequences of this for how we write?

1   This character of theoretical writing is necessary, for we need to elaborate different kinds of conceptual space in order to throw the everyday world into question, to think about it differently so that it may be possible to change it.

2   The 'real world' is not especially transparent to everyone who moves around in it, and there is a good deal of theoretical reflection – different ways of describing things that are strange and disturbing to researchers.

3   We need to treat every different kind of audience who might read a research report as a peculiar 'subculture' with its own linguistic peculiarities and ways of making sense of what is going on within their own frames of reference.

4   The member of an assessment panel, user of a psychology service, sponsor of a funding body, administrator in a health service or academic journal editor all look for a kind of writing that will speak to *them* in *their* language.

One way of meeting these competing demands is to provide the reader with different ways in to the research, and in some of the best research there are different abstracts that are tailored to different audiences (e.g. Harper 1999a, 1999b).

Writing (so the audience can read and respond)

We can now turn to the structure of a 'typical' report, but this outline should be read with care, for there are always particular and peculiar preferences that different institutions have and what they like to see included and where. Each aspect should be talked through with a supervisor.

The four main sections follow the format of a traditional laboratory-experimental report. The Introduction should commence with a sentence outlining the key themes, include a review of existing research on the topic that narrows down to specific aspects, include a review of methodological possibilities that narrows down to make a case for that which is most relevant, and conclude with an outline of research questions. Each element of the Introduction should be clearly marked with subheadings. The Introduction should sell the topic and the methodology to the reader, making a case for why this is interesting, why it is worth studying and why this is a good way to go about studying it (so you should save qualms and shortcomings of the research to the Discussion). The Method section should describe how the material studied was chosen or co-researchers were contacted, what that material or who those co-researchers were, and the key stages in the production of the analysis. What is usually termed 'procedure' in this section of the report is an opportunity in radical research to emphasize that the work tracks the *process* of doing the research rather than simply implementing a predefined sequence of actions. Possible numbered appendix items should be mentioned for each of these aspects.

The Analysis section should begin with a sentence outlining what the elements will be, introductory explanations drawing attention to key aspects, quotes from the research material clearly identified with links to an appendix, and summaries indicating what is to be particularly noted. Each aspect of the analysis should be clearly marked with subheadings. The Discussion should be a mirror image of the Introduction (each element clearly marked with subheadings). Start with a sentence outlining the key themes, review what has been presented in the analysis, linking back to existing research on the topic mentioned in the Introduction, review the methodological choices that were made and possible shortcomings with the research, and conclude with an outline of conclusions and possible areas of future research arising from the study. The Discussion should reflect on what has been done and demonstrate an awareness that things could have been done differently. You may want to number these main sections and give secondary numbers to subsections (so that the first main section of the Analysis section, for example, would be 3.1, and more detailed subsections may be marked with additional numbers, 3.1.1, 3.1.2 and so on), and you may be advised to start each of these four main sections on a fresh page of the report. Layers of headings can be marked by putting the four main section headings in capital letters, subheadings within the sections in bold (and, if necessary, more detailed subsections within these in italics).

There are elements of the report that are usually best written last. In the case of the reflexive analysis you need to be clear why you have chosen to put this as the final subheading of the Analysis section or as part of the Discussion, and to make sure that it includes reflection on the actual material presented in the analysis with some indication as to how your position as researcher may have led to certain things happening or certain interpretations being made. The report may need an abstract, and here you need to check that it includes a sentence or two on the topic, material studied or co-researchers involved, method, key aspects of the analysis, conclusions and implications. You may be required to give keywords, and here you should make sure that there are words that highlight the topic, specific method, material studied or co-researchers and theories drawn upon in the Introduction and Discussion (and sometimes there is a requirement that these words are different from those that appear in the title). It is important that the title of the report accurately reflects what the study is about, promising only what can be delivered in the report.

Only list those references at the end of the report that you have actually read. If you include a reference in the main text that has been cited by someone else that you have read, you mark this in the text by saying that so and so was cited by the actual author that you read – for example, 'Bloggs argued so and so (cited in Blagg 1995)', and then you only put 'Blagg (1995)' with the full reference in the reference list. References should follow a consistent format, and one good style guide is provided by the British Psychological Society (2003). Use this guide, which follows in key respects that of the American Psychological Association, unless you are specifically advised to do otherwise (you will see that internet resources, of which this is one, have particular referencing conventions so that the reader is able to see when the relevant website was accessed). Appendices should be numbered, and you should make sure that these are mentioned at relevant points in the main text. For some good examples of undergraduate reports see Willig (2001).

The possible space for creative writing in a research report will vary from institution to institution (an issue that is addressed in Box 11.2), and this space is always bounded by the overall structure of the report (for which the parameters are summarized in the form of a checklist in Box 11.3 – see p. 155).

Box 11.2 *Open questions about creative writing*

One major difference between qualitative research reports and writing in mainstream laboratory-experimental psychology is that you are encouraged to write in the first person. But this use of 'I' leads us to consider aspects of the research that are not usually valued by psychology. Each invitation to creative writing in a research report also contains within it some temptations to self-indulgence that need to be carefully thought through. Proposals for criteria for assessing good writing (Richardson 2000: 937) open up possibilities, but are there also some risks in these suggestions as well?

1   *Substantive contribution to our understanding of a phenomenon* – the use of the personal pronoun does help draw attention to the particular position of the researcher, and this can reveal another new perspective on the phenomenon that is the subject of study. The risk is that if I simply tell you that this is what I thought without showing you how I arrived at my ideas you have to take it all on good faith.

2   *Aesthetic considerations* – the reader positioning her or himself in the text can open up possibilities for more enjoyable writing, and for introducing personal background into the study that can be illuminating. The risk is that if I am only concerned with making the report into something poetic I might be so carried away by this that I forget to tell you exactly what I did and what other people made of it.

3   *Reflexivity woven into the production of knowledge* – it is entirely possible to include reflexive commentary in every section of the report, rather than confining it to the reflexive analysis section, and this can give more depth to the report. The risk is that if I painstakingly tease apart every aspect of the study as I describe it to you, all you actually will be left with is the sense of a tortured soul agonizing about how difficult it all was.

4   *The impact of the work* – personal testimony by the researcher about the process of carrying out the research and a discussion of how they have changed as a result of it can be a way of showing the value of the work. The risk is that if I only tell you what it meant for me, you will have no evidence that anything changed for anyone else, or that anyone else is important.

5   *An embodied sense of lived experience* – showing how the personal stakes in the research played themselves out in the relationships with co-researchers or the engagement with the research material can be a way of conveying to the reader what it was like to be involved in the process. The risk is that what I experienced might be quite irrelevant to the actual study I am supposed to be describing to you.

The inclusion of research subjectivity and reflection upon the position of the researcher in qualitative research – something that is explicitly high-lighted in the 'reflexive analysis' section of the report – should also include reflection on what it will be helpful for the reader to know in order to make sense of what is described.

From the same (old things that comfort and limit)

The advantage of a 'typical' report structure is that the reader knows what to expect, and here we must also have an eye to the vexed question of criteria in qualitative research. (Chapter 10 set out a rationale for specific criteria that would be flexible and open enough for innovative work in qualitative research.) A good way to turn the typical report into something a little different is to tackle the question of 'relevance' in research head-on.

First, you can include in your Discussion some considerations about policies that might emerge from the research, to make explicit the ways in which someone reading the research report might put the ideas into practice. This can be deepened by setting out the different ways in which the research might be taken up and elaborated by specific groups.

Second, you can be clear about what needed to be adapted in the methods that you used, and what you have learned about those methods in the process of doing the research. This can be deepened by showing what the advantages and disadvantages of the method were and showing in what ways you had to develop your own version of the method in order to do the research.

Third, you can explore what the limits were to your research, but take care not to limit this account to complaints about lack of time or the problems of a small sample. You can deepen this account by showing how the assumptions you made about the research had to change as you went about it, and what other possible accounts might be given about the research process.

Box 11.3 *Explicating the parameters for a good report*

These points itemize the key components of a report, and it is worth using this as a checklist so that you can, at the very least, be clear as to why you may not want to include all of them.

1 *Title?* Accurate, informative about topic and methodology, showing awareness of the limited domain of the material studied and claims to be made?

2 *Abstract?* Topic, material or co-researchers, method, analysis, conclusions and implications?

3 *Keywords?* Topic, method, material or co-researchers, theoretical terms?

4 *Introduction?* Existing research, methodological possibilities, research questions?

5 *Method?* Material or co-researchers, how chosen, contacted and engaged with, key analytic stages?

6 *Analysis?* Elements, explanations, quotes, appendix links, summaries?

7 *Reflexive analysis?* Position as researcher, link to material in analysis?

8 *Discussion?* Topic, methodology, conclusions?

9 *References?* Consistent, inclusive?

10 *Appendices?* Numbered, mentioned at appropriate points in the main text?

To the other (new questions that disturb and change)

The disadvantage of a 'typical' report structure is that key aspects of radical qualitative research may be muted or obscured altogether. The deliberate reflexive-progressive 'action research' aspect of the work is something that should not suddenly disappear when the work is being written up, for it is going to be a study that aims to make a difference it should also 'prefiguratively' be aiming to make a difference to the ways that research is reported and read in psychology. (Chapter 9 makes the case that all research is action research in one way or another.) So, how can we take forward this 'action' aspect of the work to disturb, challenge and perhaps change taken-for-granted academic, professional and disciplinary practices? Different methodologies open up different possible questions for the way a report might be written, so let us briefly look at these in turn.

Ethnography is an ideal setting for the researcher to speak in the first person, and the ethnographic description of a community or life-world should make the analysis section of the report into an engaging story about how the researcher made sense of things. The subversive twist in this kind of work can take place in the writing of the report, when you can start to look at how we are usually expected to describe things in the strange community that is psychology and what limits are set by that community on the way we might understand the other worlds outside it.

Interviewing is an opportunity to engage in depth with someone about a topic of psychological importance, and also to trace the ways in which someone might come to think differently about things that are usually taken for granted in psychology. The outline of the topic as it is traditionally understood in psychology will be a very important part of the report, as the contract with co-researchers will be, particularly as unexpected aspects of the interaction should be attended to. The subversive twist in this kind of work appears in the reflection on the relationship between interviewer and interviewee, for here in microcosm is the relationship between psychological expert and people who are not usually treated as 'experts upon their own lives'.

Narrative approaches are an opportunity for exploring how identities are constructed and how they can also be questioned. The subversive twist in this work comes about as narratives of psychological research also become part of the topic in the writing of the report. Discourse analysis allows us to shift attention from the place where psychologists usually think the interesting stuff is (inside the head) to the different forms of language that we use to describe the world and make sense of our own place in it. The subversive twist in this research appears in the reflection on psychology itself as a set of discourses about psychology rather than deep underlying truths about human behaviour.

Psychoanalysis provides an opportunity for discussion of the place of psychological ideas in culture, and there is room for speculation about how specific aspects of psychoanalytic theory might be used for interpreting a text and for how psychoanalytic notions come to pervade the text. The subversive twist in this research appears in the report when we show the way psychoanalytic accounts contrast with psychological models and we start to explore what the relation is between psychology and the everyday world of common-sense explanations for psychological phenomena.

Other qualitative methods in psychology raise other specific questions about the way the discipline approaches human action and experience, and there are consequences for how the research is written up (e.g. Seale 1999).

Box 11.4 *Don't stop there! Beyond the report*

The best research goes beyond the report, and the writing of the report may be the least important aspect of the work.

1   You should honour any commitment made to consult with those you involved about what is included in the report.

2   Feedback should be given to those who participated about what happened to the report, and discussion about the possibilities and limits of this form of work can then be encouraged.

3   The work can be published in wider public forums so that it might stimulate reflection and change.

Of course the evaluation of the report is important, and at a certain moment in your career path through a degree or when completing a piece of funded research all of these issues about the writing of the report have to be taken seriously, but the actual written report will most likely gather dust on a shelf once it is read and assessed. The work only has a useful life if you keep it alive yourself in the world outside. If you really want to make a difference, you do so with those you have been working with *outside* the institution (e.g. Prilleltensky and Nelson 2002).

Psychology research reports pretend to open a window onto things that were done and new things that were discovered about the world. One of the strange things about qualitative research is that the researcher is an active self-reflexive agent in the construction of the things that were found, and to be true to this aspect of the research brings them face to face with some difficult ethical questions when those things have to be written up. Just as every method I have described in this book has to be modified in order to make it work for the particular research questions you are interested in exploring, so every piece of writing should be slightly different from the 'typical' report, and the little innovations you bring into your writing will introduce something new into psychology. It is exactly at the point when you challenge the reader that you can take the opportunity to make your own stamp on qualitative psychology and turn it into radical research.

Further reading

Burman, E. (1998) Disciplinary apprentices: 'qualitative methods' in student psychological research, *International Journal of Social Research Methodology*, 1(1): 25–45.

Seale, C. (1999) *The Quality of Qualitative Research*. London: Sage.

Smith, D. (1990) *Texts, Facts, and Femininity: Exploring the Relations of Ruling*. London: Routledge.

References

Adorno, T.W. (1973) *Negative Dialectics*. New York: Seabury Press.

Ahmed, B. (2000) The social construction of racism: the case of second generation Bangladeshis, *Journal of Community and Applied Social Psychology*, 10: 33–48.

Andersen, R. (1988) *The Power and the Word: Language, Power and Change*. London: Paladin.

Anderson, B. (1991) *Imagined Communities: Reflections on the Origin and Spread of Nationalism*, revised edn (original published 1983). London: Verso.

Ashcroft, B., Griffiths, G. and Tiffin, H. (eds) (1995) *The Post-Colonial Studies Reader*. London: Routledge.

Atkinson, M. and Heritage, J. (eds) (1984) *Structures of Social Action: Studies in Conversation Analysis*. Cambridge: Cambridge University Press.

Augé, M. (1995) *Non-Places: Introduction to an Anthropology of Supermodernity* (original published 1992, trans. J. Howe). London: Verso.

Badiou, A. (2001) *Ethics: An Essay on the Understanding of Evil* (original published 1998, trans. P. Hallward). London: Verso.

Badiou, A. (2002) On the truth-process. http://www.egs.edu/faculty/badiou/badiou-truth-process-2002.html (accessed 17 May 2004).

Bakhtin, M. (1981) *The Dialogical Imagination*. Austin, TX: University of Texas Press.

Bakhtin, M. (1984) *Rabelais and his World*. Bloomington, IN: Indiana University Press.

Barthes, R. (1973) *Mythologies*. London: Paladin.

Batsleer, J., Burman, E., Chantler, K., McIntosh, H.S., Pantling, K., Smailes, S. and Warner, S. (2002) *Domestic Violence and Minoritization: Supporting Women to Independence*. Manchester: Women's Studies Research Centre, Manchester Metropolitan University.

Bennett, T. (1979) *Formalism and Marxism*. London: Methuen.

Bhaskar, R. (1986) *Scientific Realism and Human Emancipation*. London: Verso.

Bhavnani, K.-K. and Phoenix, A. (eds) (1994) *Shifting Identities, Shifting Racisms: A Feminism & Psychology Reader*. London: Sage.

Billig, M. (1977) The new social psychology and 'fascism', *European Journal of Social Psychology*, 7: 393–432.

Billig, M. (1978) *Fascists: A Social Psychological View of the National Front*. London: Harcourt Brace Jovanovich.

Billig, M. (1979) *Psychology, Racism and Fascism*. Birmingham: Searchlight. http://www.ferris.edu/isar/archives/billig/homepage.htm (accessed 9 February 2004).

Billig, M. (1988) Methodology and scholarship in understanding ideological explanation, in C. Antaki (ed.) *Analysing Everyday Explanation: A Casebook of Methods*. London: Sage.

Billig, M. (1994) Repopulating the depopulated pages of social psychology, *Theory & Psychology*, 4(3): 307–35.

Billig, M. (1995) *Banal Nationalism*. London: Sage.

Billig, M. (1999) *Freudian Repression: Conversation Creating the Unconscious*. Cambridge: Cambridge University Press.

Billington, T. (2000) *Separating, Losing and Excluding Children: Narratives of Difference*. London: RoutledgeFalmer.

Bingham, W. and Moore, B. (1959) *How to Interview*. New York: Harper International.

Blackman, L. (2001) *Hearing Voices: Contesting the Voice of Reason*. London: Free Association Books.

Bowers, J. (1996) Hanging around and making something of it: ethnography, in J. Haworth (ed.) *Psychological Research: Innovative Methods and Strategies*. London: Routledge.

Bracken, P. and Thomas, P. (2001) Postpsychiatry: a new direction for mental health, *British Medical Journal*, 322: 724–7.

British Psychological Society (2003) *Style Guide*. http://www.bps.org.uk/documents/StyleGuide.pdf (accessed 14 November 2003).

Brydon-Miller, M. and Tolman, D. (eds) (1997) Transforming psychology: interpretive and participatory research methods (special issue), *Journal of Social Issues*, 53(4).

Buck-Morss, S. (1977) *The Origin of Negative Dialectics: Theodor W. Adorno, Walter Benjamin, and the Frankfurt Institute*. Hassocks: Harvester Wheatsheaf.

Buckle, A. and Farrington, D. (1994) Measuring shoplifting by systematic observation: a replication study, *Psychology, Crime & Law*, 1: 135–41.

Burkitt, I. (1991) *Social Selves: Theories of the Social Formation of Personality*. London: Sage.

Burman, E. (1990) *Feminists and Psychological Practice*. London: Sage (available on www.discourseunit.com).

Burman, E. (1992a) Feminism and discourse in developmental psychology: power, subjectivity and interpretation, *Feminism & Psychology*, 2(1): 45–59.

Burman, E. (1992b) Identification and power in feminist therapy: a reflexive history of a discourse analysis, *Women's Studies International Forum*, 15(4): 487–98.

Burman, E. (1994a) *Deconstructing Developmental Psychology*. London: Routledge.

Burman, E. (1994b) Interviewing, in P. Banister, E. Burman, I. Parker, M. Taylor and C. Tindall (1994) *Qualitative Methods in Psychology: A Research Guide*. Buckingham: Open University Press.

Burman, E. (1996) The crisis in modern social psychology and how to find it, *South African Journal of Psychology*, 26(3): 135–42.

Burman, E. (1997) Minding the gap: positivism, psychology and the politics of qualitative research, *Journal of Social Issues*, 53(4): 785–803.

Burman, E. (1998a) *Deconstructing Feminist Psychology*. London: Sage.

Burman, E. (1998b) Disciplinary apprentices: 'qualitative methods' in student psychological research, *International Journal of Social Research Methodology*, 1(1): 25–45.

Burman, E. (2003) Narratives of 'experience' and pedagogical practices, *Narrative Inquiry*, 13(2): 269–86.

Burman, E. (2004a) Organising for change? Group-analytic perspectives on a feminist action research project, *Group Analysis*, 37(1): 91–108.

Burman, E. (2004b) Discourse analysis means analysing discourse: some comments on Antaki, Billig, Edwards and Potter 'Discourse analysis means doing analysis: A critique of six analytic shortcomings', *Discourse Analysis Online*. http://www.shu.ac.uk/daol/articles/open/2003/003/burman2003003-t.html (accessed 9 February 2004).

Burman, E. (forthcoming) Engendering culture in psychology, *Theory & Psychology*.

Burman, E., Aitken, G., Alldred, P., Allwood, R., Billington, T., Goldberg, B., Gordo López, A., Heenan, C., Marks, D. and Warner, S. (1996) *Psychology Discourse Practice: From Regulation to Resistance*. London: Taylor & Francis.

Butler, J. (1993) *Bodies That Matter: On the Discursive Limits of 'Sex'*. London: Routledge.

Cameron, D. (1995) *Verbal Hygiene*. London: Routledge.

Capdevila, R. (2003) Marginality and methodology: negotiating legitimacy, *ISTP*, June.

Castaneda, C. (1970) *The Teachings of Don Juan: A Yaqui Way of Knowledge* (original published 1968). Harmondsworth: Penguin.

(charles), H. (1992) Whiteness – the relevance of politically colouring the 'non', in H. Hinds, A. Phoenix and J. Stacey (eds) *Working Out: New Directions of Women's Studies*. Lewes: Falmer Press.

Clifford, J. and Marcus, G. (eds) (1986) *Writing culture: The Poetics and Politics of Ethnography*. Berkeley, CA: University of California Press.

Collins, C. (2003) 'Critical psychology' and contemporary struggles against neo-liberalism', *Annual Review of Critical Psychology*, 3: 26–48.

Cooke, B. and Kothari, U. (eds) (2001) *Participation: The New Tyranny?* London: Zed Books.

Crawford, J., Kippax, S., Onyx, J., Gault, U. and Benton, P. (1992) *Emotion and Gender: Constructing Meaning from Memory*. London: Sage.

Crossley, M. (2000) *Introducing Narrative Psychology: Self, Trauma and the Construction of Meaning*. Buckingham: Open University Press.

Curt, B. C. (1994) *Textuality and Tectonics: Troubling Social and Psychological Science*. Buckingham: Open University Press.

Davies, B. (2000) *A Body of Writing 1990–1999*. Walnut Creek, CA: AltaMira Press.

Denzin, N. and Lincoln, Y. (eds) (2000) *Handbook of Qualitative Research*, 2nd edn. London: Sage.

Desai, A. (2002) *We Are the Poors: Community Struggles in Post-Apartheid South Africa*. New York: Monthly Review Press.

Dorling, D. and Simpson, S. (eds) (1999) *Statistics in Society: The Arithmetic of Politics*. London: Arnold.

Drury, J. (2003) What critical psychology can('t) do for the 'anti-capitalist movement', *Annual Review of Critical Psychology*, 3: 88–113.

Duckett, P. and Pratt, R. (2001) The researched opinions on research: visually impaired people and visual impairment research, *Disability & Society*, 16(6): 815–35.

Dunker, C. (forthcoming) Truth structured like fiction: sexual theories of children viewed as narrative, *Journal for Lacanian Studies*.

Elliott, R., Fischer, C.T. and Rennie, D.L. (1999) Evolving guidelines for publication of qualitative research studies in psychology and related fields, *British Journal of Clinical Psychology*, 38: 215–29.

Ellis, C. and Bochner, A. P. (2000) Autoethnography, personal narrative, reflexivity, in N.K. Denzin and Y.S. Lincoln (eds) *Handbook of Qualitative Research*, 2nd edn. Thousand Oaks, CA: Sage.

Engels, F. (1884) *The Origin of the Family, Private Property and the State*. New York: Pathfinder Press.

Evans, R. (2002) Ethnography of teacher training: mantras for those constructed as 'other', *Disability & Society*, 17(1): 35–43.

Fals Borda, O. (ed.) (1998) *People's Participation: Challenges Ahead*. Bogotá: Tercer Mundo.

Fanon, F. (1967) *The Wretched of the Earth*. Harmondsworth: Penguin.

Fanon, F. (1970) *Black Skin White Masks: The Experiences of a Black Man in a White World*. London: Paladin.

Feyerabend, P. (1975) *Against Method: analytical index and concluding chapter*. http://www.marxists.org/reference/subject/philosophy/works/ge/feyerabe.htm (accessed 15 March 2004).

Finch, J. (1984) 'It's great to have someone to talk to': ethics and politics of interviewing women, in C. Bell and H. Roberts (eds) *Social Researching: Politics, Problems, Practice*. London: Routledge.

Finlay, L. and Gough, B. (eds) (2003) *Reflexivity: A Practical Guide for Researchers in Health and Social Sciences*. Oxford: Blackwell.

Forrester, J. (1980) *Language and the Origins of Psychoanalysis*. London: Macmillan.

Foster, D. and Louw-Potgieter, J. (eds) (1991) *Social Psychology in South Africa*. Johannesburg: Lexicon.

Foucault, M. (1970) The order of discourse, in R. Young (ed.) *Untying the Text: A Post-Structuralist Reader*. London: Routledge & Kegan Paul.

Foucault, M. (1977) *Discipline and Punish: The Birth of the Prison* (original published 1975). London: Allen Lane.

Foucault, M. (1979) *The History of Sexuality, Volume I: An Introduction* (original published 1976). London: Allen Lane.

Freeman, J. (1996) *The Tyranny of Structurelessness*. http://www.hartfordhwp.com/archives/45/112.html (accessed 16 February 2004).

Freeman, M. (1993) *Rewriting the Self: Memory, History, Narrative*. London: Routledge.

Freire, P. (1972) *Pedagogy of the Oppressed*. Harmondsworth: Penguin.

Freud, S. (1914) On narcissism, in A. Richards (ed.) (1984) *On Metapsychology: The Theory of Psychoanalysis*, Pelican Freud Library Vol. 11. Harmondsworth: Pelican.

Frosh, S. (2002) *After Words: The Personal in Gender, Culture and Psychotherapy*. Houndmills: Palgrave Macmillan.

Frosh, S., Phoenix, A. and Pattman, R. (2001) *Young Masculinities*. Houndmills: Palgrave Macmillan.

Gegenstandpunkt (2003) *Warning, Communism is not Exactly Dead!* www.gegenstandpunkt.com/english/en_index.html (accessed 16 February 2004).

Georgaca, E. (2001) Voices of the self in psychotherapy: a qualitative analysis. *British Journal of Medical Psychology*, 74: 223–36.

Georgaca, E. (2003) Exploring signs and voices in the therapeutic space, *Theory & Psychology*, 13(4): 541–60.

Gillies, V., Harden, A., Johnson, K., Reavey, P., Strange, V. and Willig, C. (2004) Women's collective constructions of embodied practices through memory work: Cartesian dualism in memories of sweating and pain, *British Journal of Social Psychology*, 43(1): 99–112.

Glaser, B. and Strauss, A. (1967) *The Discovery of Grounded Theory: Strategies for Qualitative Research*. New York: Aldine.

Goffman, E. (1971) *The Presentation of Self in Everyday Life* (original published 1959). Harmondsworth: Pelican.

Good, P. (2001) *Language for those who have nothing: Mikhail Bakhtin and the Landscape of Psychiatry*. New York: Kluwer Press.

Goodley, D. and Lawthom, R. (eds) (2004) *Psychology and Disability: Critical Introductions and Reflections*. London: Palgrave.

Goodley, D. and Parker, I. (eds) (2000) Action research (special issue), *Annual Review of Critical Psychology*, 2.

Gordo López, A.J. and Cleminson, M.R. (1999) Queer science/queer psychology: a biosocial inoculation project, *Theory & Psychology*, 9(2): 282–8.

Gordo López, A.J. and Cleminson, M.R. (2004) *Techno-Sexual Landscapes: Changing Relations Between Technology and Sexuality*. London: Free Association Books.

Gordo López, A.J. and Parker, I. (eds) (1999) *Cyberpsychology*. London: Macmillan.

Gough, B., Lawton, R., Madill, A. and Stratton, P. (2003) *Guidelines for the Supervision of Undergraduate Qualitative Research in Psychology*. http://www.psychology.ltsn.ac.uk/reports.html (accessed 27 October 2003).

Granada, H. (1991) Intervention of community social psychology: the case of Colombia, *Applied Psychology: An International Review*, 40(2): 165–80.

Gubrium, J. and Silverman, D. (eds) (1989) *The Politics of Field Research*. London: Sage.

Hamer, B. (dir.) (2003) *Kitchen Stories (Salmer fra Kjøkkenet)*. Oslo: Bent Hamer Studio.

Harding, S. (ed.) (1987) *Feminism and Methodology: Social Science Issues*. Bloomington, IN: Indiana University Press.

Harper, D. (1999a) Deconstructing paranoia: an analysis of the discourses associated with the concept of paranoid delusion. Unpublished PhD thesis, Manchester Metropolitan University. http://www.criticalmethods.org/thesis0.htm (accessed 2 February 2004).

Harper, D. (1999b) Tablet talk and depot discourse: discourse analysis and psychiatric medication, in C. Willig (ed.) *Applied Discourse Analysis: Social and Psychological Interventions*. Buckingham: Open University Press.

Harper, D. (2003) Developing a critically reflexive position using discourse analysis, in L. Finlay and B. Gough (eds) *Reflexivity: A Practical Guide for Researchers in Health and Social Sciences*. Oxford: Blackwell.

Harper, D. (2004) Storying policy: constructions of risk in proposals to reform UK mental health legislation, in B. Hurwitz, V. Skultans and T. Greenhalgh (eds) *Narrative Research in Health and Illness*. London: BMA Books.

Harré, R. (1979) *Social Being*. Oxford: Basil Blackwell.

Harré, R. (1984) Some reflections on the concept of 'social representation', *Social Research*, 51(4): 927–38.

Harré, R. (2004) Staking our claim for qualitative psychology as science, *Qualitative Research in Psychology*, 1: 3–14.

Harré, R. and Secord, P.F. (1972) *The Explanation of Social Behaviour*. Oxford: Blackwell.

Hartsock, N. (1987) The feminist standpoint: developing the ground for a specifically feminist historical materialism, in S. Harding (ed.) *Feminism and Methodology: Social Science Issues*. Bloomington, IN: Indiana University Press.

Haug, F. (ed.) (1987) *Female Sexualisation*. London: Verso.

Haug, F. (2000) Memory work: the key to women's anxiety, in S. Radstone (ed.) *Memory and Methodology*. Oxford: Berg.

Hebdige, D. (1979) *Subculture: The Meaning of Style*. London: Methuen.

Henley, N. (1979) *Body Politics: Power, Sex, and Nonverbal Communication*. Englewood Cliffs, NJ: Prentice Hall.

Henriques, J., Hollway, W., Urwin, C., Venn, C. and Walkerdine, V. (1984) *Changing the Subject: Psychology, Social Regulation and Subjectivity*. London: Methuen.

Henwood, K., Griffin, C. and Phoenix, A. (eds) (1998) *Standpoints and Differences: Essays in the Practice of Feminist Psychology*. London: Sage.

Hine, C. (2000) *Virtual Ethnography*. London: Sage.

Hirschkop, K. and Shepherd, D. (eds) (2001) *Bakhtin and Cultural Theory*, revised and expanded 2nd edn. Manchester: Manchester University Press.

Hobsbawm, E. and Ranger, T. (eds) (1983) *The Invention of Tradition*. Cambridge: Cambridge University Press.

Hoens, D. and Pluth, E. (2004) What if the other is stupid? Badiou and Lacan on 'logical time', in P. Hallward (ed.) *Think Again: Alain Badiou and the Future of Philosophy*. London: Continuum Books.

Hollway, W. (1989) *Subjectivity and Method in Psychology: Gender, Meaning and Science*. London: Sage.

Hollway, W. and Jefferson, T. (2000) *Doing Qualitative Research Differently: Free Association, Narrative and the Interview Method*. London: Sage.

Holzman, L. (ed.) (1999) *Performing Psychology: A Postmodern Culture of the Mind*. London: Routledge.

Holzman, L. and Morss, J. (eds) (2000) *Postmodern Psychologies, Societal Practice and Political Life*. London: Routledge.

Hook, D. (2001) Discourse, knowledge and materiality: Foucault and discourse analysis, *Theory & Psychology*, 11(4): 521–47.

Hook, D. (2004) Fanon and the psychoanalysis of racism, in D. Hook (ed.) with N. Mkhize, P. Kiguwa and A. Collins (section eds) and E. Burman and I. Parker (consulting eds) (2004) *Critical Psychology*. Cape Town: UCT Press.

Hook, D. and Vrdoljak, M. (2002) Gated communities, heterotopia and a 'rights' of privilege: a 'heterotopology' of the South Africa security-park, *Geoforum*, 33: 195–219.

House, R. (2002) *Therapy Beyond Modernity: Deconstructing And Transcending Profession-Centred Therapy*. London: Karnac Books.

Howitt, D. and Owusu-Bempah, J. (1994) *The Racism of Psychology: Time for Change*. New York: Harvester Wheatsheaf.

Hunt, J. C. (1989) *Psychoanalytic Aspects of Fieldwork* (Sage University Paper Series on Qualitative Methods, Vol. 18). Beverley Hills, CA: Sage.

Illich, I. and Sanders, B. (1988) *The Alphabetization of the Popular Mind*. London: Marion Boyars.

Irvine, J., Miles, I. and Evans, J. (eds) (1979) *Demystifying Social Statistics*. London: Pluto Press.

Jacoby, R. (1977) *Social Amnesia: A Critique of Conformist Psychology from Adler to Laing*. Hassocks: Harvester Press.

James, A. (2001) *Raising Our Voices: An Account of the Hearing Voices Movement*. Gloucester: Handsell Publishing.

Jiménez-Domínguez, B. (1996) Participant action research, in I. Parker and R. Spears (eds) *Psychology and Society: Radical Theory and Practice*. London: Pluto Press.

Jones, P. (2004) Discourse and the materialist conception of history: critical comments on critical discourse analysis, *Historical Materialism*, 12(1): 97–125.

Kagan, C. and Burton, M. (2000) Prefigurative action research: an alternative basis for critical psychology?, *Annual Review of Critical Psychology*, 2: 73–87.

Khan, R. (1987) *Down the Road, Worlds Away*. London: Virago.

Kitzinger, C. (1987) *The Social Construction of Lesbianism*. London: Sage.

Kitzinger, C. (2000) Doing feminist conversation analysis, *Feminism & Psychology*, 10(2): 163–93.

Kitzinger, C. and Wilkinson, S. (1996) Theorizing representing the other, in S. Wilkinson and C. Kitzinger (eds) *Representing the Other: A Feminism & Psychology Reader*. London: Sage.

Kitzinger, C. and Wilkinson, S. (1997) Validating women's experience? Dilemmas in feminist research, *Feminism & Psychology*, 7(4): 566–74.

Kubrick, S. (dir.) (1960) *Spartacus* (restored 1991). Hollywood: Universal Pictures.

Kvale, S. (1996) *InterViews: An Introduction to Qualitative Research Interviewing*. London: Sage.

Lacan, J. (1979) *The Four Fundamental Concepts of Psycho-Analysis*. Harmondsworth: Penguin.

Laplanche, J. and Pontalis, J. B. (1988) *The Language of Psychoanalysis*. London: Karnac Books and the Institute of Psycho-Analysis.

Lasch, C. (1978) *The Culture of Narcissism: American Life in an Age of Diminishing Expectations*. New York: Norton.

Lather, P. (1995) The validity of angels: interpretive and textual strategies in researching the lives of women with HIV/AIDS, *Qualitative Inquiry*, 1(1): 41–68.

Lévi-Strauss, C. (1963) *Structural Anthropology.* New York: Basic Books.

Lewin, K. (1946) Action research and minority problems, *Journal of Social Issues,* 2: 34–46.

Livia, A. (1996) Daring to presume, in S. Wilkinson and C. Kitzinger (eds) *Representing the Other: A Feminism & Psychology Reader.* London: Sage.

Loewenthal, D. (2004) Psychotherapy, ethics and citizenship: 'When the other is put first, how to position oneself?', *Psychodynamic Practice,* 10(1): 121–5.

McAdams, D. (1993) *The Stories we Live By: Personal Myths and the Making of the Self.* New York: Morrow.

McLaughlin, K. (2003) Agency, resilience and empowerment: the dangers posed by a therapeutic culture, *Practice,* 15(2): 45–58.

McLaughlin, T. (1996) Hearing voices: an emancipatory discourse analytic approach, *Changes: An International Journal of Psychology and Psychotherapy,* 14(3): 238–43.

McLaughlin, T. (2003) From the inside out: the view from democratic psychiatry, *European Journal of Counselling, Psychotherapy and Health,* 6(1): 63–6.

Maclure, M. (2003) *Discourse in Educational and Social Research.* Buckingham: Open University Press.

Madge, C. and Harrison, T. (1939) *Mass-Observation: The Science of Ourselves.* Harmondsworth: Penguin.

Malone, K. and Friedlander, S. (eds) (2000) *The Subject of Lacan: A Lacanian Reader for Psychologists.* New York: State University of New York Press.

Marcus, G.E. (1986) Contemporary problems of ethnography in the modern world system, in J. Clifford and G. Marcus (eds) *Writing culture: The Poetics and Politics of Ethnography.* Berkeley, CA: University of California Press.

Marks, D., Burman, E., Burman, L. and Parker, I. (1995) Collaborative research into education case conferences, *Educational Psychology and Practice,* 11(1): 41–8.

Marsh, P., Rosser, E. and Harré, R. (1974) *The Rules of Disorder.* London: Routledge & Kegan Paul.

Martin-Baró, I. (1994) *Writings for a Liberation Psychology* (trans. A. Aron and S. Corne). Cambridge, MA: Harvard University Press.

Marx, K. (1845) Concerning Feuerbach, in New Left Review (ed.) (1975) *Karl Marx: Early Writings.* Harmondsworth: Pelican.

Maso, I. (2003) Necessary subjectivity: exploiting researchers' motives, passions and prejudices in pursuit of answering 'true' questions, in L. Finlay and B. Gough (eds) *Reflexivity: A Practical Guide for Researchers in Health and Social Sciences.* Oxford: Blackwell.

Mather, R. (2000) The foundations of critical psychology, *History of the Human Sciences,* 13(2): 85–100.

Melancholic Troglodytes (eds) (2003) Anti-capitalism (special issue), *Annual Review of Critical Psychology*, 3.

Middleton, D. and Edwards, D. (eds) (1991) *Collective Remembering*. London: Sage.

Mitchell, J. (1974) *Psychoanalysis and Feminism*. Harmondsworth: Penguin.

Mkhize, N. (2004) Sociocultural approaches to psychology: dialogism and African conceptions of the self, in D. Hook (ed.) with N. Mkhize, P. Kiguwa, P. and A. Collins (section eds) and E. Burman and I. Parker (consulting eds) *Critical Psychology*. Cape Town: UCT Press.

Monk, G., Winslade, J., Crocket, K. and Epston, D. (eds) (1997) *Narrative Therapy in Practice: The Archaeology of Hope*. San Francisco: Jossey-Bass.

Montero, M. and Fernández Christlieb, P. (eds) (2003) Critical psychology in Latin America (special issue), *International Journal of Critical Psychology*, 8.

Moore, M., Sixsmith, J. and Knowles, K. (eds) (1996) *Children's Reflections on Family Life*. London: Falmer Press.

Morawski, J. (1997) The science behind feminist research methods, *Journal of Social Issues*, 53(4): 667–81.

Morgan, D. (1981) Men, masculinity and the process of sociological inquiry, in H. Roberts (ed.) *Doing Feminist Research*. London: Routledge & Kegan Paul.

Morgan, J., O'Neill, C. and Harré, R. (1979) *Nicknames: Their Origins and Social Consequences*. London: Routledge & Kegan Paul.

Moscovici, S. (1976) *La Psychanalyse: Son Image et Son Public*, 2nd edn. Paris: Presses Universitaires de France.

Moscovici, S. (1984) The phenomenon of social representations, in R.M. Farr and S. Moscovici (eds) *Social Representations*. Cambridge: Cambridge University Press.

Murphy, E., Dingwall, R., Greatbach, D., Parker, S. and Watson, P. (1998) Qualitative research methods in health technology assessment: a review of the literature, *Health Technology Assessment*, 2(16). www.nechta.org (accessed 18 November 2003).

Murray, C. and Sixsmith, J. (1998) E-mail: a qualitative research medium for interviewing? *International Journal of Social Research Methodology*, 1(2): 103–21.

Newman, F. (1999) Beyond narrative to performed conversation ('In the beginning' comes much later), in L. Holzman (ed.) *Performing Psychology: A Postmodern Culture of Mind*. London: Routledge.

Newman, F. and Holzman, L. (1993) *Lev Vygotsky: Revolutionary Scientist*. London: Routledge.

Newman, F. and Holzman, L. (1997) *The End of Knowing: A New Developmental Way of Learning*. London: Routledge.

Nightingale, D. (1999) Bodies: reading the body, in I. Parker and the Bolton Discourse Network *Critical Textwork: An Introduction to Varieties of Discourse and Analysis*. Buckingham: Open University Press.

Nightingale, D.J. and Cromby, J. (eds) (1999) *Social Constructionist Psychology: A Critical Analysis of Theory and Practice*. Buckingham: Open University Press.

Ochs, E. (1979) Transcription as theory, in E. Ochs and B.B. Shiefflen (eds) *Developmental Pragmatics*. London: Academic Press.

Orbach, S. (1999) *The Impossibility of Sex*. London: Faber & Faber.

Parker, I. (1989) *The Crisis in Modern Social Psychology, and How to End It*. London: Routledge (available on www.discourseunit.com).

Parker, I. (1992) *Discourse Dynamics: Critical Analysis for Social and Individual Psychology*. London: Routledge (available on www.discourseunit.com).

Parker, I. (1994a) Qualitative research, in P. Banister, E. Burman, I. Parker, M. Taylor and C. Tindall *Qualitative Methods in Psychology: A Research Guide*. Buckingham: Open University Press.

Parker, I. (1994b) Reflexive research and the grounding of analysis: social psychology and the psy-complex, *Journal of Community and Applied Social Psychology*, 4(4): 43–66.

Parker, I. (1994c) Discourse analysis, in P. Banister, E. Burman, I. Parker, M. Taylor and C. Tindall *Qualitative Methods in Psychology: A Research Guide*. Buckingham: Open University Press.

Parker, I. (1996) The revolutionary psychology of Lev Davidovich Bronstein, in I. Parker and R. Spears (eds) *Psychology and Society: Radical Theory and Practice*. London: Pluto Press.

Parker, I. (1997) *Psychoanalytic Culture: Psychoanalytic Discourse in Western Society*. London: Sage.

Parker, I. (1998) Constructing and deconstructing psychotherapeutic discourse, *European Journal of Psychotherapy, Counselling and Health*, 1(1): 77–90.

Parker, I. (1999a) Critical psychology: critical links, *Radical Psychology: A Journal of Psychology, Politics and Radicalism*. www.yorku.ca/faculty/academic/danaa/index.htm (accessed 3 February 2003).

Parker, I. (1999b) Qualitative data and the subjectivity of 'objective' facts, in D. Dorling and L. Simpson (eds) *Statistics in Society: The Arithmetic of Politics*. London: Arnold.

Parker, I. (ed.) (1999c) *Deconstructing Psychotherapy*. London: Sage.

Parker, I. (1999d) Tracing therapeutic discourse in material culture. *British Journal of Medical Psychology*, 72(4): 577–87.

Parker, I. (2002) *Critical Discursive Psychology*. New York: Palgrave Macmillan.

Parker, I. (2003a) Discursive resources in the Discourse Unit, *Discourse Analysis Online*, 1(1): http://www.shu.ac.uk/daol/articles/v1/n1/a2/parker2002001.html (accessed 29 October 2003).

Parker, I. (2003b) Psychoanalytic narratives: writing the self into contemporary cultural phenomena, *Narrative Inquiry*, 13(2): 301–15.

Parker, I. (2003c) Jacques Lacan, barred psychologist, *Theory & Psychology*, 13(1): 95–115.

Parker, I. (2004a) Discursive practice: analysis, context and action in critical research, *International Journal of Critical Psychology*, 10: 150–73.

Parker, I. (2004b) Psychoanalysis and critical psychology, in D. Hook (ed.) with N. Mkhize, P. Kiguwa and A. Collins (section eds) and E. Burman and I. Parker (consulting eds) *Critical Psychology*. Cape Town: UCT Press.

Parker, I. (forthcoming) Lacanian ethics in psychology: seven paradigms, in A. Gülerce, A. Hofmeister, J. Kaye, G. Saunders and I. Steauble (eds) *Theoretical Psychology*. Toronto: Captus Press.

Parker, I. and the Bolton Discourse Network (1999) *Critical Textwork: An Introduction to Varieties of Discourse and Analysis*. Buckingham: Open University Press.

Parker, I. and Burman, E. (1993) Against discursive imperialism, empiricism and constructionism: thirty-two problems with discourse analysis, in E. Burman and I. Parker (eds) *Discourse Analytic Research: Repertoires and Readings of Texts in Action*. London: Routledge (available on www.discourseunit.com).

Parker, I. and Spears, R. (eds) (1996) *Psychology and Society: Radical Theory and Practice*. London: Pluto Press.

Parker, I., Georgaca, E., Harper, D., McLaughlin, T. and Stowell Smith, M. (1995) *Deconstructing Psychopathology*, London: Sage.

Parkes, M.B. (1992) *Pause and Effect: An Introduction to the History of Punctuation in the West*. London: Scolar Press.

Phoenix, A. (1987) Theories of gender in black families, in G. Weiner and M. Arnot (eds) *Gender Under Scrutiny*. Basingstoke: Hutchinson.

Phoenix, A. (1994) Practising feminist research: the intersection of gender and 'race' in the research process, in M. Maynard and J. Purvis (eds) *Researching Women's Lives from a Feminist Perspective*. London: Taylor & Francis.

Potter, J. (1996) *Representing Reality: Discourse, Rhetoric and Social Construction*. London: Sage.

Potter, J. and Edwards, D. (2003) Sociolinguistics, cognitivism and discursive psychology, *International Journal of English Studies*, 3: 93–109.

Potter, J. and Hepburn, A. (2003) 'I'm a bit concerned' – early actions and psychological constructions in a child protection helpline, *Research on Language and Social Interaction*, 36(3): 197–240.

Potter, J. and Wetherell, M. (1987) *Discourse and Social Psychology: Beyond Attitudes and Behaviour*. London: Sage.

Pratt, R., Burman, E. and Chantler, K. (2004) Towards understanding domestic violence: reflections on the research and the 'domestic violence and minoritization' project, *Journal of Community and Applied Social Psychology*, 14: 33–43.

Prilleltensky, I. (1994) *The Morals and Politics of Psychology: Psychological Discourse and the Status Quo*. Albany, NY: State University of New York Press.

Prilleltensky, I. and Nelson, G. (2002) *Doing Psychology Critically: Making a Difference in Diverse Settings*. New York: Palgrave Macmillan.

Psathas, G. (1995) *Conversation Analysis: The Study of Talk-in-Interaction*. Thousand Oaks, CA: Sage.

Reason, P. and Bradbury, H. (eds) (2001) *Handbook of Action Research: Participative Inquiry as Practice*. London: Sage.

Reason, P. and Rowan, J. (eds) (1981) *Human Inquiry: A Sourcebook of New Paradigm Research*. Chichester: Wiley.

Reicher, S. (2000) Against methodolatry: some comments on Elliott, Fischer and Rennie, *British Journal of Clinical Psychology*, 39: 1–6.

Richardson, L. (2000) Writing: a method of inquiry, in N.K. Denzin and Y.S. Lincoln (eds) *Handbook of Qualitative Research*, 2nd edn. London: Sage.

Rinehart, R. (1998) Fictional methods in ethnography: believability, specks of glass, and Chekhov, *Qualitative Inquiry*, 4(2): 200–24.

Roiser, M. (1974) Asking silly questions, in N. Armistead (ed.) *Reconstructing Social Psychology*. Harmondsworth: Penguin.

Rose, N. (1985) *The Psychological Complex: Psychology, Politics and Society in England 1869–1939*. London: Routledge & Kegan Paul.

Rose, N. (1996) *Inventing Ourselves: Psychology, Power and Personhood*. Cambridge: Cambridge University Press.

Rosenhan, D.L. (1973) On being sane in insane places, *Science*, 179: 250–8.

Roth, S. and Epston, M. (1996) Consulting the problem about the problematic relationship; an exercise for experiencing a relationship with an externalized problem, in M.F. Hoyt (ed.) *Constructive Therapies II*. New York: Guilford.

Rowbotham, S., Segal, L. and Wainwright, H. (1979) *Beyond the Fragments: Feminism and the Making of Socialism*. Newcastle: NSC/ICP.

Said, E. (1985) *Orientalism*. Harmondsworth: Penguin.

Salmon, P. (2003) How do we recognise good research? *The Psychologist*, 16(1): 24–7.

Sampson, E.E. (1993) *Celebrating the Other: A Dialogical Account of Human Nature*. New York: Harvester Wheatsheaf.

Samuels, A. (1993) *The Political Psyche*. London: Routledge.

Saussure, F. de (1974) *Course in General Linguistics*. Glasgow: Fontana/Collins.

Seale, C. (1999) *The Quality of Qualitative Research*. London: Sage.

Shaw, W. (1994) *Spying in Guru Land: Inside Britain's Cults*. London: Fourth Estate.

Sixsmith, J. and Murray, C. (2001) Ethical issues in the documentary date analysis of internet posts and archives, *Qualitative Health Research*, 11(3): 423–32.

Smith, D. (1990) *Texts, Facts, and Femininity: Exploring the Relations of Ruling*. London: Routledge.

Smith, J., Flowers, P. and Osborn, M. (1997) Interpretative phenomenological analysis and the psychology of health and illness, in L. Yardley (ed.) *Material Discourses of Health and Illness*. London: Routledge.

Spencer, L., Ritchie, J., Lewis, J. and Dillon, L. (2003) *Quality in Qualitative Evaluation: A Framework for Assessing Research Evidence*. www.policy-hub.gov.uk (accessed 24 November 2003).

Spender, D. (1980) *Man Made Language*. London: Routledge.

Spradley, J. (1979) *The Ethnographic Interview*. New York: Holt, Rinehart & Winston.

Squire, C. (1990) Crisis, what crisis? Discourses and narratives of the 'social' in social psychology, in I. Parker and J. Shotter (eds) *Deconstructing Social Psychology*. London: Routledge (available on www.discourseunit.com).

Squire, C. (1995) Pragmatism, extravagance and feminist discourse analysis, in S. Wilkinson and C. Kitzinger (eds) *Feminism and Discourse*. London: Sage.

Squire, C. (ed.) (2000) *Culture in Psychology*. London: Routledge.

Stephenson, N. (2003) Rethinking collectivity: practising memory-work, *International Journal of Critical Psychology*, 8: 160–76.

Strauss, A. and Corbin, J. (1990) *Basics of Qualitative Research: Grounded Theory Procedures and Techniques*. London: Sage.

Terre Blanche, M. and Durrheim, K. (eds) (1999) *Research in Practice: Applied Methods for the Social Sciences*. Cape Town: UCT Press.

Tindall, C. (1994) Issues of evaluation, in P. Banister, E. Burman, I. Parker, M. Taylor and C. Tindall (1994) *Qualitative Methods in Psychology: A Research Guide*. Buckingham: Open University Press.

Tuhiwai Smith, L. (1999) *Decolonizing Methodologies: Research and Indigenous Peoples*. London: Zed Books.

Vaillant, G.E. (1971) Theoretical hierarchy of adaptive ego mechanisms: a 30-year follow-up of 30 men selected for psychological health, *Archives of General Psychiatry*, 24: 107–18.

Walker, T. (1988) Whose discourse?, in S. Woolgar (ed.) *Knowledge and Reflexivity: New Frontiers in the Sociology of Knowledge*. London: Sage.

Walkerdine, V. (1990) *Schoolgirl Fictions*. London: Verso.

Walkerdine, V. (ed.) (1996) *Feminism & Psychology Reader: Class*. London: Sage.

Watson, K. (forthcoming) Queer theory, *Group Analysis*,

Wetherell, M. and Potter, J. (1992) *Mapping the Language of Racism: Discourse and the Legitimation of Exploitation*. London: Harvester Wheatsheaf.

White, M. (1989) The process of questioning: a therapy of literary merit? In *Selected Papers*. Adelaide: Dulwich Centre Publications.

White, M. (1995) *Re-Authoring Lives: Interviews and Essays*. Adelaide: Dulwich Centre Publications.

Wilbraham, L. (2004) Discursive practice: analysing a *Lovelines* text on sex and communication for parents, in D. Hook (ed.) with N. Mkhize, P. Kiguwa and A. Collins (section eds) and E. Burman and I. Parker (consulting eds) *Critical Psychology*. Cape Town: UCT Press.

Wilkinson, S. (1988) The role of reflexivity in feminist psychology, *Women's Studies International Forum*, 11(5): 493–502.

Wilkinson, S. (1998) Focus groups in health research: exploring the meanings of health and illness, *Journal of Health Psychology*, 3(3): 329–48.

Wilkinson, S. and Kitzinger, C. (eds) (1996) *Representing the Other: A Feminism & Psychology Reader*. London: Sage.

Williamson, J. (1978) *Decoding Advertisements: Ideology and Meaning in Advertising*. London: Marion Boyars.

Willig, C. (ed.) (1999) *Applied Discourse Analysis: Social and Psychological Interventions*. Buckingham: Open University Press.

Willig, C. (2001) *Introducing Qualitative Research in Psychology: Adventures in Theory and Method*. Buckingham: Open University Press.

Willis, P. (1980) *Learning to Labour: How Working Class Kids Get Working Class Jobs* (original published 1977). Aldershot: Gower.

Wilson-Tagoe, N. (2003) Representing culture and identity: African women writers and national cultures, *Feminist Africa*, 2: 25–41.

Yardley, L. (ed.) (1997) *Material Discourses of Health and Illness*. London: Routledge.

Index

APPROACHES TO PSYCHOLOGY
4th Edition
William Glassman and Marilyn Hadad

Review of the Third Edition
"Nowhere else is there such thorough coverage of the major perspectives in their historical context. Glassman's clear, consistent and utterly coherent style provides interest through anecdotes, fables, everyday experiences and concrete psychological research examples."
The Times Higher Education Supplement

This revised and expanded edition of *Approaches to Psychology* builds on the wide appeal of the earlier editions. It explains what the discipline of psychology is, how it developed and how it can contribute to the understanding of human behaviour and experience.

This book introduces students to the five major conceptual frameworks or "approaches" to psychology: **biological, behaviourist, cognitive, psychodynamic and humanistic.** The methods, theories and assumptions of each approach is explored so that the reader builds an understanding of psychology as it applies to human development, social and abnormal behaviour.

New to this edition:
- Brand new layout with more illustrations and two colour design
- Case studies that run throughout the book
- Increased coverage of social psychology
- Enhanced treatment of cross-cultural issues
- New work on evolutionary psychology
- Online Learning Centre (OLC) with student support material, instructor test bank (www.openup.co.uk/glassman)

Features:
- Overview of key methods of psychological research
- Student friendly pedagogy including discussion points and queries, clear chapter summaries, key terms and concepts defined in context
- Annotated suggestions for further reading
- Extensive glossary and bibliography

This clear and concise exploration of psychology is key reading for students new to the discipline.

Contents*: List of Illustrations - Preface - Behaviour and psychology - The Biological approach - The behaviourist approach - The cognitive approach - The psychodynamic approach - The humanistic approach - Perspectives on d development - Perspectives on social behaviour - Perspectives on abnormal behaviour - Psychology in perspective - Appendix - Research mehods and statistics - Glossary - References - Index.*

512pp   0 335 21348 0 (Paperback)

HEALTH PSYCHOLOGY: A TEXTBOOK
Third Edition
Jane Ogden

Praise for this edition:
"This third edition...provides a clear, comprehensive and up-to-date overview of a wide range of research and theory...it clearly deserves to maintain its place as the number one choice of health psychology textbook." John Weinman, King's College, London

Health Psychology: A Textbook has made a major contribution to the teaching and study of this rapidly expanding discipline. Maintaining its strong review of theory and research, the third edition has been substantially revised to provide increased coverage of the biological aspects of health and illness. This book now provides the most accessible and comprehensive guide to the field.

The new two-colour layout has been designed with students in mind, including clear illustrations, boxed discussion points, and specific research boxes. Many new features have been incorporated into this edition to further aid students and teachers, including:

· Additional, entirely new chapter on stress; now two chapters address this key topic
· Expanded and improved section on psychoneuroimmunology (PNI)
· Expanded chapter on pain
· New section on the consequences of coronary heart disease (CHD) and rehabilitation of CHD patients
· New chapter on eating behaviour
· New coverage of problems associated with social cognition models

Health Psychology: A Textbook is essential reading for all students and researchers of health psychology and for students of medicine, nursing and allied health courses.

Contents:

Detailed table of contents - List of figures and table - Preface to third edition - Technology to enhance learning and teaching - Acknowledgements - An Introduction to Health Psychology - Health Beliefs - Illness Cognitions - Doctor-patient communication and the role of health professionals' health beliefs - Smoking and alcohol use - Eating behaviour - Exercise - Sex - Screening - Stress - Stress and illness - Pain - Placebos and the interrelationship between beliefs, behaviour and health - HIV and cancer: psychology throughout the course of illness (1) - Obesity and coronary heart disease: psychology throughout the course of illness (2) - Measuring health status: from mortality rates to quality of life - The assumptions of health psychology - Methodology glossary - References - Index.

352pp   0 335 21471 1 (Paperback)   0 335 21487 8 (Hardback)